WHATEVER'S GOING TO BECOME OF US?

WHATEVER'S GOING TO BECOME OF US?

THE STORY OF ONE BOY'S STRUGGLE FROM POVERTY TO SUCCESS

TERRY HOPLEY

CONTENTS

Gawd 'Elp Us	7	The Cotswolds	105
The Musical Hopleys	13	Tomatoes, What a Nuisance!	107
We Won the War in 1944	18	Stupid Englishman!	111
Peace	24	La Palma	114
Staying the Course	30	A Recipe for Disaster	123
The Life of a Reporter	33	The Needles Club	130
The Path to Success	38	The Golden Years	135
Love and Loss	44	Man Overboard	140
Providing	47	Around the Edges	146
National Service	50	Out of the Blue	152
The Little Girl I Fell For	54	Business, As Usual	155
Fun and Games	57	Nobody Kicks Me Twice	161
A Cut Above	59	Set for Life	164
Wedded Bliss	62	In Exile	168
The Hammers	65	Thanks for the Memories	171
Life in the Fast Lane	69	Aches and Pains	178
In Love Again	75	Sanctuaries	183
Selling Space	82	Back at Sea	187
Welcome Aboard	87	These Days	195
Sea Sickness	90	An Answer to the Question	197
My Sea Change	96	And So Life Goes On	199
Fourwinds	101		

GAWD 'ELP US

"Whatever's going to become of us?" my mother sobbed. Her tears carved tiny pink streams in the powdered plaster that covered her face, as she clutched the four of us to her ample bosom. We had heard the bomb coming, starting with the drone of the German aircraft above us then gradually developing an increasing whine that meant it would probably find a target nearby. I can remember the noise, but I was too young to consider the consequences of the Luftwaffe's nightly terror campaign. Sandwiched between my sisters, Jessie and Sheila, and with my brother, Sam, mum and our neighbour Mrs Popkin and her children keeping the nightly air raid vigil in our bomb shelter, I felt strangely protected. I had little idea, until later, that the bombs were bringing death and destruction. In fact, it was to be years before I realised just how dangerous a time my early childhood was. Staccato bursts of anti-aircraft fire, the whining and grinding of overhead aircraft and the surreal sight of barrage balloons – silver behemoths waiting to intercept German planes – were just a familiar part of my early childhood. They were as much part of it as a Friday-night teaspoon of cod liver oil or a dash to O'Dell's sweet wagon when we heard he had reject fruit drops 'off the ration'.

The bomb shelter in the backyard of our London County Council estate home in Sheppey Road, Dagenham, consisted of a narrow doorway set into a mound of piled up soil. Earthen steps slunk down into a congested two-by-three-metre white-washed chamber. In the adventurous spirit of childhood, I kind of preferred to drift off to sleep in the shelter's dank candle-lit recesses, surrounded by my family, than in the tiny bedroom I shared with my brother. My sister Jessie, who was old enough to recognise that this was no adventure, squeezed my hand as a God-almighty roar shook the street and flakes of plaster cracked from the ceiling, showering our upturned faces. "Gawd 'elp us," exclaimed Mrs Popkin, once the quaking had stopped. My mother, her hands trembling as she patted my hair, simply wailed her daily war cry: "Whatever's going to become of us?"

We heard it again when the all-clear siren sounded and we clambered out of the shelter to find the glass blown from the windows, littering the cabbages growing in our backyard like exploded stars. All the doors and a big section of the roof had also been blown off. Mum also muttered it again, sadly, when she first saw us off for evacuation. In fact, I heard that phrase almost daily throughout my childhood. She (and we) had no way then of knowing that what would become of us was something more than any of us could ever have dreamed.

We had been evacuated once already, in 1939, at the start of the war, before the Blitz began. I remember little about our journey to the stately home of the Weston-Stevens family in Maidenhead, but the evacuation was my first introduction to a political balls-up – sending us kids away when the skies were clear and then bringing us back again when the bombs began falling. In truth, it made little difference to Dagenham, which was already a target for the Luftwaffe thanks to important installations such as the docks, the power station, and Ford, as well as the Hornchurch aerodrome. Then came the Blitz – an eight-month campaign during which London was bombed for 57 consecutive nights, leaving 375,000 homeless and more than 37,000 dead. By the time we returned to Dagenham from Maidenhead, air raids punctuated the nights. We would often emerge from the shelter in the morning to find giant smoking craters where a neighbour's house or business used to be. With a child's naïve invincibility, I never felt at risk of death, even in the midst of the mayhem, but given the scenes of devastation on our doorstep we were soon evacuated again. Our second evacuation is clearer in my memory, but, typically, we were back home again before the attacks made by ominous doodlebugs and V2 rockets, the latter of which weighed 13 tonnes and travelled so fast they plundered entire neighbourhoods before anyone even heard them coming or had a chance to run.

"Sam, Jessie, make sure you look after Sheila and Terry. Now, don't cry darling. And be good. It's very kind of these people to take you in, so mind your manners." My mother fussed and flapped, firmly attaching the name labels that identified us four Hopley kids, making sure we had all packed our meagre belongings properly, and wiping away my tears as we boarded the lorry that would transport us to Paddington Station and away to god-knows-where. Thankfully, mum was allowed to accompany us to the station, which was teeming with worried mothers, tearful children and the occasional soldier. I still remember staring at the enormous black steam engine with a mixture of fear and awe. Crowded maroon carriages trailed behind it, all packed with children. Some of the older kids were no doubt relishing the adventure and anxiously waiting to break into the brown paper bags that carried sandwiches for the journey. Others pressed runny noses up against the glass as they waved to their mums on the platform – all these stiff-upper lipped British matrons were reduced to tears wondering when they would see their little darlings again.

It was the longest train trip I had ever been on, and the novelty wore thin after a few hours. Once Jessie and Sam had allowed us to consume our drinks and sandwiches and we'd chugged on past Swindon to the small village of Purton in Wiltshire, we were more than ready to get off.

"Terry, grab your case," my elder sister Jessie, who was always my protector, shuffled me out of the carriage. Sam put on a brave face; he was painfully shy so left most of the interacting to the girls. We were shepherded off the train and all walked together to the local church hall. All of the kind families that had agreed to take evacuees were gathered there. They walked among us as if at a market, taking their pick. The four of us stood together, dutifully being appraised, aware that we were not considered a good choice because of our number. However, our friends the Dudleys (Dolly, George and little Roy) were even less likely to be chosen, largely because underneath Roy's label, scrawled in humiliating bold capital letters, were the words 'WETS BED'. Poor Roy! Luckily he didn't recognise the indignity, after all he was only two at the time.

When the Dudleys were eventually chosen they stayed in Purton for only a short time before they were evacuated to Newton-Flotman in Norfolk. No family was willing to take all four of us Hopley children, so my sisters and I went with Mr and Mrs Price to 14 The Peak, Purton. Sam was taken by himself to stay with another family.

I had been taken back to Dagenham a few times during my evacuation and was always distraught at having to return to Purton, even though Mr and Mrs Price were undoubtedly kind to us. "Don't cry Terry. Come on now" mum placated me as I clung to her skirts and howled. Godfrey and Tony, Mr and Mrs Price's two boys, looked on with embarrassment and Jessie tried to entice me with any number of 'distractions', but I was having none of it – I wanted to go home. It was even harder when my mum took us back to Purton and then had to say goodbye. "Look, Terry. Look at what Tony's got," Mrs Price pointed to the cunning little Hornby train set, wending its way around the track. I was transfixed. My tears dried up in a flash and I was immediately over there, winding the little clockwork engine and setting the carriage on the track.

"Well, at least give me a kiss goodbye," mum smiled. She obviously agreed to the ploy, and I was suddenly very happy to see her off, all the while coveting the little engine. Still, no sooner had mum turned the corner than Mrs Price scooped up the train set and back it went into its box, where it would remain for the rest of my time at Purton. I was never allowed to play with it again. It was a long time before I forgot that.

At the time, I couldn't understand why, if we had to go and stay with anyone, it couldn't be one of my grandmothers. They both lived in Stepney, which would have afforded us no protection at all, but I loved them both, despite their many differences.

Nanny Hopley was one of the true characters of the East End.

"What do you call this?" she would menace, her tight, steel-grey bun bobbing as she socked the butcher with a right hook and slapped the joint of unsatisfactory meat he had sold her down on the counter. Shopkeepers in Stepney were understandably terrified of my heavily tattooed, sailor-swearing grandmother, and most stayed out of her way. I could see why – I'd seen her punch them on several occasions and developed a wary admiration for her toughness. She was of the race of hard-working cockney women. She could neither read nor write, so when it came to administrative matters requiring her to sign her name, she rolled up her sleeves to expose her carbolic soap-scrubbed, raw-looking hands and laboriously scrawled an erratic X. Years of obsessive-compulsive cleaning had probably contributed to her red, shiny complexion and sandpapery hands. She was fanatically fastidious. Every day, to the chagrin of her neighbours, she dragged her furniture out in the street and scrubbed her tiny house from top to bottom. On finishing the task, she dragged it all inside again and proceeded to carefully scrub the pavement. This behaviour, coupled with her criticism of her neighbours' slovenly habits, led to a good many arguments (even some that ended in fisticuffs) but people eventually learned that they could not win against my nan and took her insults philosophically. Despite her fierce reputation, she doted on us kids. Every Christmas she gave me a brand-new *Rupert the Bear* book. How I treasured those books. I read each one over and over again until I knew everything there was to know about Rupert, with his yellow check trousers, red jumper and flying scarf. Beats a playstation every time when you let your imagination do the work!

Nanny Bubbles, true to her nickname, was the exact opposite – a bubbly, fecund woman who was always keen to attend my parents' parties, quite literally with bells on! Why the garter she kept her stockings up with was adorned with tinkling bells I have no idea, but her frivolity probably went some way towards explaining why she had so many children. Nanny Bubbles continued having kids well into middle age, giving us some uncles and aunties that were younger than we were. In fact, she got her nickname because our young Aunty Eileen used to sit in the pram blowing bubbles, so we called her "bubbles", which led to her mother eventually being given that nickname too. It stuck, and we called her Nanny Bubbles until she died at the age of 96.

Nanny Bubbles was an accomplished storyteller and she often regaled us with the tale of how she came face to face with Jack the Ripper. As a girl, she used to be sent out night and morning to light and extinguish the gas lamps that illuminated the streets of the East End. One dark night, as she carried out her tasks, she was bowled over by a tall toff of a gentleman who came running hastily around the corner. The man stopped and picked her up, cautioning, "A little girl like you really shouldn't be out so late lighting streetlamps". Then he put her back down, turned and sprinted off into the darkness. Minutes later, Nanny Bubbles insisted, she heard the shrill squeal of a police whistle. The next day, the East End was abuzz with the news that another prostitute had been murdered the night before.

Was it really a close encounter with the infamous Jack the Ripper? We will never know, but of course my nan always insisted that it was, and we always listened with horrified glee to the tale. It didn't stop her going out to light the gas lanterns though – not until she began her prolific breeding, which was not long afterwards.

Like many Londoners at the time, and especially those with lots of children, Nanny Bubbles often struggled to make ends meet so my mother and my Uncle Sonny had at one point lived in a Dr Barnardo's Home. As hard as some events in my mother's childhood were, she had inherited her mother's sunny personality and remained a five-foot-nothing party girl who could always raise a laugh. Around fifty years later, when I picked mum up to drive her to our daughter Michelle's wedding reception at the plush Stifford Lodge Hotel, mum went very quiet as we drove through the gates.

"I have been here before!" she exclaimed. "This was the Dr Barnardo's I lived in when I was a little girl." At first, my wife Jean and I thought it was just her memory playing tricks on her, but when we checked we found out that the hotel had indeed once been a Dr Barnardo's Home. If only someone could have told my mum way back then: "Don't worry, one day you'll be driven here again in the back of your son's Rolls Royce!"

THE MUSICAL HOPLEYS

"Turn right over on your right side Alice,
Your knees are sticking in me Crystal Palace,
Dear o' Lor',
I'm nearly on the floor,
I'm only hanging on by my right side now,
So let's have a little bit more."

Sheila's strong voice rose above all of ours, even though I stood up on a chair to make sure I could be heard and seen among all of the other party guests (I always did like to be the centre of attention!). Despite the war and tight rations, my family life was a merry one and nearly every Saturday night my parents' friends from the Roundhouse pub, the Ship and Shovel and the Thatched House would gather at our house for a party. Fortunately, we were all a bit too young to understand the more ribald sentiment in some of the songs we joined in with, but we enjoyed it all the same, screaming out:

"At our party everyone was drunk,
They were giving us lots of gin,
Lumps of toffee with almonds in,
As I was doing a jig I got an awful shock,
Old Maria fell in the fire,
And burnt her almond rock."

We were a musical family. Our living room was crowded with instruments, on which we regularly thrashed out enthusiastic tunes and held impromptu singalongs that inspired mum to lead us in a tap dance on the lino. I was lucky because I was the youngest, so I was spoilt with a weekly piano lesson with Mrs Simpson. She discovered I had an affinity for music and by the time I was eleven, I had progressed through to grade seven in the Royal Academy of Music exams. My sister Sheila was, in truth, even more musically talented than I was, and no doubt would have done better than I given the same opportunity, but I was privileged to be the one receiving the lessons. Unfortunately, although I was later offered a scholarship to the Royal Academy, we had to turn it down because we couldn't afford it. I only wish I could play even half as well now. Sadly, I let my music slip and it now feels blasphemous for me to even touch the elegant grand pianos that grace the living rooms of my homes in England, France and Australia. Mind you, it was undoubtedly, the far less affluent living room in our old house in Sheppey Road that inspired my love for music. It was a living room perfectly designed for kids. The piano, drums, piano accordion, trumpet and ukulele all vied for space with a large punching bag that dangled from the ceiling.

On party nights, a great keg of beer jostled for a corner and kept everyone in good spirits, even my Uncle Terry, who had inherited Nanny Hopley's pugilistic tendencies. Uncle Terry was the instigator of the boxing bag and passed some of his expertise on to me, teaching me how to punch…and how to punch hard. He was a stoker in the Royal Navy, a dedicated brawler who was built like a bull and had a temper to match. Barely a week went by without him flattening one of the neighbours or anyone else who disagreed with him. When he couldn't find anyone to fight, he would take himself off to the local fairground to earn a fiver by knocking out the regular hard man in the boxing booth. However, he was fiercely loyal and always acted as if he were the protector of all of us – and he usually was. I particularly loved him because he was my namesake, so I was known as "Little Terry" throughout my childhood. There was only one person in the world he was afraid of – his big brother, my dad. Strangely, for all dad's quiet, old-school ways, I could see why Uncle Terry was afraid of him. It was dad who taught me the occasional necessity of giving someone a right-hander early in the argument, at least before they gave you one (although, it was possibly Uncle Terry who had taught him that as a kid). One day when I was about twelve, the local insurance man rudely pushed me off my perch on the front gate as he hurried inside to collect his weekly shilling. I angrily told dad, who dryly responded,

"Did he now? Well you should've whacked him one." You can imagine the look of surprise on the face of the man from the "Pru" when I chased after him and thumped him.

"That's the way, Son," encouraged dad, smiling.

I didn't realise it at the time, but I was extremely fortunate to have a dad who worked in a protected occupation as a lorry driver for the Co-op, delivering flour. At first, when my mates George and Roy Dudley, Jimmy Woodhouse and Arthur Pither told exotic tales of their dads' heroics fighting the Germans or the Japanese, I felt guilty that my dad was home every night. But when Arthur's dad died, followed by Jimmy's dad, and with Mr Dudley away in Burma for most of the war, I began to count my blessings. I doted on my quiet, strict dad and my favourite childhood memory is of him.

"Come on and give your old dad a cuddle," he'd urge of a Saturday afternoon. I was the youngest and probably the most spoilt, but I had already reached the age where cuddling your parents was considered a bit naff, so I would hold out.

"Oh, come on, Terry," he'd persist. "Come give me a cuddle and I'll give you a shilling."

I used to love my Saturday afternoon cuddles, curled up with dad for a nap – not only did I get dad's rare affection, but I also got paid for it. It seemed the ideal situation. I also used to love wiping the gluggy, congealed strings of flour out of his eyes when he returned home from work, as well as acting as his personal butler, waiting on him while he ate his dinner. One afternoon, he had stopped in at Petticoat Lane and bought a large piece of salt fish, his favourite meal. Mum lovingly served it up and I set about doing my duty.

"Can you get me a glass of water, please, Son?" dad would request and I would dash out and bring it back for him in a milk bottle, because we didn't have any glasses.

"Salt," dad commanded, and I ran out to the larder, returning with seasoning.

"Vinegar please, Terry," and off I hurried again to fetch it, feeling very important. At the time, rations were strict and everything was conserved.

"Did you have to fill up the vinegar bottle from a jar of pickled beetroot?" Dad chastised mum, holding up the bottle he'd just liberally poured over his dinner. "The whole lot's gone pink!"

Unfortunately, the fault was mine. Dad had just doused his fish in a prize bottle of cherry brandy my parents had been saving for Christmas. My days of playing butler to dad were over!

Although rations were in place during the war, our family enjoyed a quality of life that I can appreciate more as the years go by. Every Christmas we would hang up our stockings in anticipation of receiving an orange, or, even better, a banana; tropical fruit was rarer than sweets. Later, the house teemed with family and friends, all enthusiastically joining in a singalong. The singalongs continued long after the war when we obtained our first wind-up gramophone and were able to singalong with the inimitable Max Bygraves, my mum's secret heartthrob. What a shame she had passed on before he became my next door neighbour and great pal. When Max himself died it left a big hole in our lives. Every year my mother would sigh as she reluctantly set about plucking a chicken for Christmas dinner. It was a job she was not particularly keen on – even less so after one offensive half-plucked cockerel leapt off the draining board with a loud squawk, prompting mum to squeal "Whatever's going to become of us?" in shock. She never did believe dad's explanation that the unfortunate bird was dead but its nervous system was still active. After that incident, she waited a good few hours after they'd been killed to ensure they were dead before she plucked them.

It certainly didn't pay to be a cockerel in Dagenham in those days. As was the case for many families during the war, chickens were our main defence against hunger. They roamed the shed, were the scurge of our carefully kept gardens, sprang unexpectedly from the privet hedge, and even hatched in a beautiful little incubator in the bedroom I shared with my brother Sam. You can imagine the thrill we got when the eggs, all lined up on cotton wool under a bright, warm light bulb, began to rock, then crack, then reveal a tiny, soaking-wet little chick. All of our neighbours brought their potato peelings and vegetable scraps to help us feed them and, in return, left our house carrying eggs. Chickens also provided a useful swap with the butcher, the greengrocer or O'Dell's Sweet Shop (my favourite), or might find their way onto the draining board themselves intended for our dinner. Mostly we would care for the chicks until they grew old enough to join the others in the "fowls' house" in the garden. Then perversely, despite lavishing careful attention on the chicks, I took a strange pleasure in later watching dad expertly wring their necks. There was something real and immediate about being involved in the first and end product of my dinner. Sometimes, dad would take young chickens to Petticoat Lane to be sold, and occasionally I was allowed to accompany him. A visit to The Lane (as Petticoat Lane was called) was an experience not to be missed. The market flourished on Sunday morning when the large Jewish fraternity that dominated the East End of London would turn up as the sellers, and thousands of cockney families would flock there, primarily as the buyers. It was chaotic, class conscious and alive. The sellers were recognised by their smart trilby hats and dark suits, the buyers by their flat caps and white scarves knotted above collarless shirts. Everything was available from black market chocolate, booze and ladies stockings to second-hand radios, bicycles and hand-me-down clothing. At one end of The Lane was Club Row, which was for livestock, or in our case deadstock, as my dad stood there with a couple of scrawny chickens waiting for the affluent Jewish men to hand over a few shillings for them.

On other occasions, I would catch the bus with mum to collect our rations.

"You've rubbed it out, I can see the outline of the pencil mark," the butcher glowered indignantly at mum, who had indeed lined up for the second time at Bob the Butcher's in Barking to collect a half shoulder of lamb.

"Don't have such a bleedin' cheek! We've been queued up here for hours. What are you talking about?" Mum bluffed, blushing in the knowledge that she had to feed our family something other than chicken somehow, even if it meant tampering with the ration book.

"All right then," the butcher acquiesced gruffly, handing over another half shoulder and again pencilling a large tick into the ration book, this time with increased pressure on the pencil. That ration books were marked off in pencil was salvation for many families. When we had got our quota, back on the bus we would go, and, once home, mum would carefully endeavour to remove the coloured mark with soap and water so we could receive our quota again. Half a shoulder of lamb didn't go far between six of us and usually it had to last. Just about everything was rationed, including sweets, and it was my burning desire to be in charge of my own sweets coupons. A converted caravan at Canonsleigh Road housed O'Dell's Sweet Shop – paradise for war children with a sweet tooth. Coupons were divided into D's (one ounce) and E's (two ounces) and the day that I was allowed to queue up with the other kids for the prize of a farthing golly bar or two ounces of liquorice allsorts was when I finally knew that my entrance into the world of the "big kids" was nigh.

WE WON THE WAR IN 1944

"Wake up, Terry. Rise and shine," Jessie pulled back the old army overcoat that served as my blanket. "First day of school, remember! Now come on and get dressed, and let's comb your hair."

Out of all of my siblings, Jessie was the one who took care of me the most, she combed my hair every morning and got me ready for school, and she even bought me my very first book. It was to be one of many. I quickly found that I enjoyed school and excelled at it, although my first day at Monteagle Primary School certainly didn't hint at my potential. It remains vivid in my memory, unfortunately for all the wrong reasons. I was terrified when I had to let go of Sheila's hand to be taken to the infants' section for the first time, but it was not long before Sheila had to return, much to her embarrassment. To be blunt I had shit myself.

"You dirty little sod Terry! What do you mean Miss Ireland told you to keep your eyes shut?" Sheila hissed, hurrying me past the window at breakneck speed in the hope that none of her friends would see us. Sheila was in junior school, and was old enough to know that her friends were not kind enough to let something as embarrassing as this pass. If they saw us, she would cop it by association.

"She…she told us to lie down on the coconut mat for a nap and to be quiet and keep our eyes closed," I sobbed, my four-year-old legs hurrying to keep up with my big sister – especially given my state, which meant I had to walk crouched over, knees knocking together to prevent further catastrophe.

"She didn't mean you couldn't open your eyes and ask to go the toilet!" Sheila rolled her eyes in exasperation, "Now hurry up before anyone sees you."

"I di…didn'…didn't know that," I wailed even louder, as a trickle of poo began to join the others that were already running out of the leg of my short trousers. By the time we had walked the two miles home the offending substance was beginning to harden on my legs. My first day at school was far from a roaring success. Thankfully, the rest of my school years passed more smoothly.

In those days in Britain, schools did not just teach you, they fed you as well, and every morning we would line up to receive our one-third of a pint of milk. At lunch, daily servings of meat, potatoes, greens and gravy were followed by lumpy semolina. School finished at 4 pm, but kids whose mothers were at work (and most mothers worked during the war years) would walk back to school in the early evening, after a few hours of playing in the streets, to grab a thick slice of bread and jam.

The war raged on during my early years at primary school. The piercing whine of the air raid siren meant we were frequently bustled into the cloakroom to play blindman's bluff until the all-clear sounded. I never did discover what protection the magical cloakroom afforded, but, fortunately, my school was never hit by a bomb. However much I enjoyed school, I do remember being sad when I heard that a neighbouring school had been blown to smithereens one night. I would like to say my sadness was in sympathy for the poor sods who had been huddled inside using the school as an air-raid shelter, but truth be told, with all the cheek of youth, I was just disappointed that the school wasn't mine! On another occasion, my friend Roy Dudley and I narrowly avoided being hit by an exploding V1 rocket as we walked home from school – an assault that remains vivid in my mind. It flew past and exploded just a few hundred yards from us, sending railings from a nearby bridge scattering in all directions and showering the street with glass and debris. With ears ringing and eyes watering from the dust, we did not need to be told not to hang around.

"Run!" I screamed at Roy, who required no encouragement. He had taken off down the street screaming "Mummmmy!" at the top of his lungs. The rocket smashed into the home of an elderly couple, obliterating their house and killing them both. The same V1 also claimed the life of one of my school friends, Charlie Mabbut. We learned at school the next day that a metal railing had shot straight through him, killing him instantly. It just as easily could have been any one of us.

How we managed to concentrate on our studies is anyone's guess, but schoolwork came easily to me and I came top of my class in almost every subject. I owe an enormous debt of gratitude to my teachers, Mr Swift, Mr Rushton, Mr Isaacs and Mr Carroll. They were quite simply brilliant teachers – and believe me, we were no angels to teach! We received encouragement when we deserved it and the cane when it was required; I was the recipient on a number of occasions. All of the aforementioned teachers disciplined me with that whippy little rod at one point or another, but I bore no grudges; in a healthy way I actually loved and respected them more for the support and discipline they gave us. As well as academic prowess, I enjoyed success on the playing fields, and with the help of pugnacious Uncle Terry, even found my way into the Essex Schools Boxing team. I also did well in the cricket team and at badminton, but oddly enough, the one sport that was to become an enormous part of my life later on – football – didn't really interest me as a child. As an adult, it would be a major contributor to my career. Monteagle was a good school, but fortunately my first pangs of ambition at that school were to go unfulfilled.

"Go on, Ivor, show him," Jimmy Woodhouse encouraged, as we all huddled down behind the school wall, crowding around to witness Ivor's amazing feat. Ivor, who had achieved immense popularity through his astounding ability to convert his winkle into a fire hose, promptly downed trunks and expertly pulled his foreskin over the end of his penis, sealing it while he peed.

"Blimey! Wow! Ha ha, get a look at that!" we would all chant admiringly, as his nether regions swelled like a water-filled balloon before the grand finale – a firm squeeze that sent a powerful jet of urine streaming over the school wall to the cheers of, "Cor, that one was at least six foot high!"

I harboured secret ambitions to achieve this amazing stunt myself for a good many months, and spent fruitless hours practising it, but all to no avail. (Oh how very different my life may have been!). At any rate, perhaps that was why we worried little about the German bombs at my school – had the Huns managed to set the school on fire, Ivor's fire hose would have put it out!

I may not have reached the upper echelons of penile manipulation, but my friends and I certainly made up for it with childish pranks and imaginative games. When most people reminisce about their childhood in England they evoke memories of snowballs shattering the crisp wintery days, or the endless, mild sunshine of the summer holidays – my memories are no different. I cannot recall the dark, grey drizzly days, but I remember plenty of fun-packed afternoons playing in the streets with my friends. During the summer holidays we would often leave the house after breakfast and not return until quite late at night, sometimes playing in our street and sometimes venturing further afield. Sometimes we even rode our old second-hand bikes to Rainham to go bird-nesting. "Up you go. That nest up the top there," urged my mate Arthur, who was usually more of a tormenter than an accomplice. He pointed to a nest that quivered uncertainly at the top of a tall tree. Jimmy and I (or David Smith or George and Roy Dudley – all of us suitable targets for Arthur's torture) would dutifully clamber to the top. Once there, the fragile eggs were carried ever so gently in our mouths for the long climb down, leaving our hands free so we could grasp the flimsy branches.

"Nice one," Arthur would smile vindictively when we reached the bottom, invariably smacking us in the mouths and splattering yolk all over our faces. Strangely, it seemed we never learned; soon enough we would be back up another tree to collect another egg.

Arthur was the main instigator of pranks too. "Tighter," he would hiss, as we pulled the near-invisible cotton thread we had tied to the knocker of No 189 Sheppey Road nice and taut, passing it through the knocker of No 188 on the opposite side of the street.

"Now you take it," I passed the end of the thread to Roy, who immediately scooted across the other side of the road to pass it through the knocker of 187. And so it went on, until we had trussed up about a dozen door-knockers and hidden ourselves in a hedge, lying in wait.

"Here comes someone," we would grin with glee, as some unsuspecting adult walked into our domino-like trap, breaking the cotton and causing simultaneous knocks at a dozen different front doors. We thought it was hilarious, but only marginally more so than seeing one of the mums in our street encounter one of our many winter snow slides. Hours were spent firmly packing down snow and ice on the pavement until we had created an excellent ice slide. We would launch ourselves at this slippery spot at full pelt, then slide gracefully for twenty to thirty yards to the applause of our watching mates. Unfortunately, mothers laden down with groceries rarely achieved our level of grace. If they were unlucky enough to step unawares on "our" section of the pavement, they usually slid disgracefully on their backsides, along with the contents of their shopping bags, cursing us kids the entire time.

Sometimes, the dangerous wide reaches of the Thames, about two miles away, would beckon to us, urging us out of our street and down to the river's edge. Barges lolled on the river, each carrying a cargo of peanuts destined for an experimental scheme known as the Groundnut Scheme, which aimed to grow peanuts in Tanzania to provide Britain with much-needed cooking oil. I still know very little about the scheme, but what I do know is that at the river an old door festooned with tin cans quickly transformed itself into a raft of Huckleberry Finn-like proportions.

"Paddle faster over that side," George reprimanded, as we splashed and paddled the unstable contraption up to a barge to help ourselves to fistfuls of peanuts. At the time, I couldn't swim a stroke and I surely would have drowned had I fallen off or had the leaky door sunk. Thankfully, our raft held up and we returned to shore to supplement our diet of peanuts with green rhubarb plucked from nearby allotments, washing the fibre-rich mass down with a pint of milk nicked from someone's doorstep. Such adventures sure kept our bowel habits regular! However, those games were mere child's play compared to some of the more daring activities we war children got up to.

"Won't work," Arthur scoffed.

"Will too!" George returned, knowing that his younger brother Roy was always clever with his hands.

"Roy'll do it," I added my opinion, passing Roy the heavy spring.

"Give us the hammer," he requested as he concentrated on pushing the spring down into the shaft of the metal tube we had found, mashing it up taut against the bit of metal that was to act as a hammer inside the "muzzle".

"Looks rubbish," laughed Arthur. "It'll never work!"

"Oh, it'll work all right," Roy assured us. "That'll work for sure," he glanced proudly at our most prized possession – a live .303 bullet he had found, which rested promisingly in George's palm. The contraption was inelegant to say the least, but at the appointed hour we convened at the end of the Dudley's garden as Roy introduced the bullet into the barrel of his home-made gun.

"Wind it right back," urged George, as Roy wound back the spring and took aim at a tin can he had placed on top of the dustbin – the target.

"Ready, aim, fire!"

BANG!

It worked all right, so well I'm amazed I'm here to tell the tale. The bullet whizzed past the intended target and, with a tremendous crack, shot right through Mr Dudley's garden shed. Its passing left a hole a foot in diameter where it entered, and another of equally impressive dimensions where it exited. Where it went after that, we never knew. As far as we are aware, it never killed anyone. Had it done so, we might have noticed because one of the less innocent games played in Dagenham during the war years involved snooping around the temporary morgue. Bodies retrieved from the rubble after the air raids on Dagenham Docks and the Barking power station were taken to a temporary repository, which consisted of an old school hall in Goresbrook Road. Death was an ever-present part of life in 1943, so it was not that surprising that we used to line up to morbidly peer through the window, seeking a glimpse of the bodies, each covered in a white sheet with an identity label dangling from an inert big toe. For some (not me I hasten to add) that dangling ID tag was just too tempting. The mischief it presented did not bear thinking about, but more than one unfortunate soul was probably sent to St Peter carrying the wrong identification. (I told you it didn't bear thinking about!)

Thankfully, no one in my family ended up in a makeshift morgue, although we had a few lucky escapes. My sister Jessie had left school to take up a position as a machinist in Aldgate, and my older brother Sam left school a year later, at the age of thirteen, to work as an apprentice barber in Commercial Road, Stepney. Working put them both at risk when attacks occurred during the day. I remember Jessie arriving home from work one day, her hair twinkling with fragments of glass as she told us that a bomb had destroyed the building next to her workplace. Sam's work was suspended at one point when, a few hours after he had left to go home, the shop suffered a direct hit and was completely demolished. Somehow, it all seemed quite normal to me and my friends, but by 1944 the tide had turned.

"We won the war in 1944!" we belted out, as we marched home from school, our boots making sparks on the road from all of the studs our parents had hammered into the soles to make them last longer. The song was a year before its time, but life in Dagenham was beginning to feel different. There was optimism in the air. Eventually, we gathered happily around our wireless to listen to our beloved Winston Churchill telling us the Germans had surrendered.

PEACE

Apart from the street parties organised to celebrate the arrival of peace, and that we no longer had to sleep in the air raid shelter, the war's end made little difference to my life. The only real change was that we no longer played blindman's bluff in the cloakroom at school. During my last two years of primary school, I made great progress, largely due to my old school teachers Mr Swift and Mr Rushton, whom I was always anxious to please, whether in the boxing ring or in English class – always my favourite subject.

At the time, I was the only Hopley kid at school, my older siblings were all at work, Sheila having recently taken up an apprenticeship as a hairdresser. The job lasted only a few months before she decided a bus conductress would be a better option. Then it was an auxiliary nurse, a shop assistant, a messenger and a cashier.

"What the bleedin' 'ell is that on your 'ead?" dad demanded to know, as Sheila arrived at the dinner table with a coil of material hiding every strand of her hair, imitating the fashionable "turban" headwear of the day.

"It's a turban and they're all the fashion. And anyway, don't worry I've started a new job. I'm an usherette."

"Usherette! Sheila that's about the tenth job you've had this year. Why can't you stick at anything? One of these days you'll get my hand round your jaw," dad threatened. Threatening a hand round the jaw of any one of the four of us, like my mum's "whatever's going to become of us?" was one of dad's oft-used phrases but it never developed beyond a threat. He loved us far too much for that.

"And get that scarf off your 'ead. You're not going out like that, young lady," dad uttered the immortal fatherly threat. My gorgeous, mischievous sister was proving quite a handful. Out of all of us Hopley kids, she was the only one dad couldn't handle, but her quick sense of humour and cheeky smile meant that everyone loved her – especially my kids in later life. Unbeknown to dad, under Sheila's glamorous headwear lurked newly bleached peroxide-blonde tresses, so I wisely shut my mouth and said nothing. Besides, I couldn't talk, I was wearing bicycle clips on my trousers to hide the fact that I had altered them to turn them into drainpipes.

"By the way, Terry," my mother added "you'd better clean up your room. Your cousin Kevin's coming to stay. Your Aunt Peg is unwell."

Uncle Terry arrived the next day, bearing their youngest son, Kevin, in his arms. Aunt Peg had contracted the dreaded tuberculosis and was hospitalised for three years, during which time Kevin was to stay with us. Barry, Kevin's older brother had been sent to live with one of my other aunts. Although only in nursery school, Kevin became like a little brother to me for those three years and I loved him dearly. He was little more than 18 months old when he arrived – a frail little boy with big brown eyes and snow-white hair. He looked like an angel, but he certainly didn't speak like one. At that age he had a very limited vocabulary, but most of the words he had picked up were swear words. He was told to call my mum auntie and, in true cockney fashion, he left out the 'n' and the 't'. The first words I recall him saying on his first morning, as he awoke in his second-hand cot, were: "Ar-ee, I ain't pissed my cot!" A true little tearaway from Peabody Buildings, Stepney, in London's East End he was! Because my mum worked full time, Kevin was dispatched to nursery school each morning and it was my responsibility to get him there on my way to school with the help of George Dudley. We used his pram as a kind of chariot, and as we roller-skated behind it we could pick up quite a lick of speed. Kevin enjoyed all this, but it was inevitable that this arrangement would one day lead to grief.

"Argggghg, @*^&% you! You effing #^&*%!," Kev squealed, as we lost control of his pram, which careered down a steep hill and overturned, shooting him thirty feet through the air, which was blue with curses. I can still see his angelic little face as he lay on the pavement, calling us names a navvy would be proud of.

The day eventually came when my Aunt Peg was released from hospital and Kevin was reunited with his brother and his mum and dad. It should have been a happy day, but it wasn't. He cried and we cried tears of genuine sorrow. We never saw much of him in the ensuing years but we did meet up again recently at the funeral of his dad, my tough Uncle Terry.

Another of my cousins, Alan – the son of my dad's sister Maggie – attended my school and, like myself, was an outstanding pupil. As it came time to leave junior school, we were both singled out for special treatment and it was not long before I stood on the doorstep, my hands beaming as I presented mum and dad with my final year report card. I knew I had done well, but I was surprised to read on my report card: "An outstanding pupil who richly deserves a scholarship." I was confident I'd done well, but, at the age of eleven, my last few months of school were beginning to be taken up with the idea of girls, rather than study. Perhaps sensibly, boys and girls' were kept separate at Monteagle Junior School, and never the twain should meet as far as teachers were concerned. However, that had not managed to thwart the pangs of pre-pubescent love I felt for Barbara Busby, who, unfortunately, showed no signs of returning my devotion, despite the many hours I spent lolling outside her house waiting for a sign. George Dudley was equally enamoured with another girl, June Fair. Nothing ever came of it, but I still remember that Barbara's birthday was three days after mine.

Despite the accolades, my report had classified me as "different" simply because I had been awarded a scholarship to High School, and I wasn't quite sure I liked the idea. I certainly felt uncomfortable about being separated from most of my mates. Dagenham at the time was a haven of homogeneity – all of the council houses looked identical, distinguished only by how tidy people kept their privet hedges. But suddenly, I was moving out of this comfort zone. Strangely, later in life I would realise that the uniformity was simply an illusion. In fact, a great many remarkable individuals lived within the identical walls of Becontree Council Estate, each starting out on a journey that would lead to fame, fortune or both. George Dudley and my other mate Georgie Carey were to go on to Bifrons Secondary Modern, and from there, on to remarkable achievements in totally different fields. Neither would have been classed as academics simply because of the school they had been sent to. George Dudley became an outstanding amateur sportsman playing more than 800 games for Dagenham Football Club. Georgie Carey surpassed the achievements of us all by becoming Archbishop of Canberbury, but more about that later. Suddenly, new doors were opening for me and I had no idea which corridor to take. Should I go for Barking Abbey Grammar (which my cousin Alan had chosen, setting him on his career path as a fighter pilot and wing commander instructor) or Dagenham County High (which Dudley Moore chose) or South East Essex County Technical High School? I had no idea. I ended up choosing my school for one reason alone – I liked the colour of their blazer the most. It was royal blue with black piping, and was complemented by a jaunty matching Just William cap. Woe betide us if we were ever seen out of school without our cap! Unhappily for me, it was the jacket, not the cap that was to be my undoing at South East Essex County Tech.

"What rubbish," dad scoffed, when he had seen the cost of the thick, hairy blazers made of out what seemed like old blanket material at the uniform shop. They itched like hell and were not particularly stylish.

"Your sister can make you one much better than this for half the cost, son," dad argued – and that was how it came about that I stood out like a sore thumb at my new school and was singled out as a cockney trouble maker. The blazer my dressmaker sister Jessie had made for me was correctly emblazoned with the school badge and had the same meticulously sewn-on black piping seen on the school's official blazer, so it was not breaking school rules. In fact, she was a skilled tailor and it looked better than the other blazers. The only difference was that it was made of gabardine, which gave it a kind of "Teddy Boy" drape. Still, the blazer, coupled with my strong cockney accent, singled me out from the other students. Many of my classmates were from posh private houses and I always felt a bit of misfit. It didn't help that most of our teachers were a useless bunch. The headmaster, Mr Arthur, usually administered a clip over the ear when I passed him in the hallway, just in case I'd been misbehaving, and Miss Williams, the senior mistress, hated me with a vengeance – then again, she hated everyone with a vengeance. Eventually, I decided if I was going to be treated as a misfit I might as well be one and set about concentrating more on my score with the opposite sex than with my score in examinations.

If you guess who is the sender,
May I undo your suspender?

I scrawled shakily in the Valentine's day card, under the mistaken belief that Mrs Ansell, our maths teacher and the object of my affection, would not identify my left-handed handwriting. I was pretty proud of myself, having made up the verse. Mrs Ansell was one of the few brilliant teachers at my senior school. She had short, cropped jet-black hair, twinkling dark eyes and lovely legs, which sat beautifully in her tight, fashionable skirt. She was also quite strict – I liked that. It was a daring enough advance to get me expelled had it been sent to anyone else.

"Thanks for the card, Hopley," was Mrs Ansell's sole reaction, whispered out of the corner of her mouth as she strolled past me in the corridor with a small smile hovering about her lips. And thank you too, Mrs Ansell, wherever you are.

My preoccupation with the fairer sex did me a big favour, although I did not notice it at the time. In our final two years of senior school we were allowed to choose two extra-curricular subjects to help us in our potential professions. Most boys chose woodwork, metalwork, technical drawing or art, but my mate Terry Higgins and I knew those classes were not where the girls would be. We chose shorthand and typing. There were six boys and thirty girls in our class – we'd hit the jackpot!

"Whatever's going to become of us?" my mother's quavering lamentation was sternly followed with, "Wait until daddy gets home," as soon as I marched in the door from school. I was in big trouble! There on the table, in front of my crying sister and my horrified mother, lay my diary. All of my adolescent fantasies were exposed for all to see. Sheila, despite her tears, wore a sneaky, gleeful expression. She had a habit of going through my personal possessions and today's haul was a good one. The diary's saucy entries were mostly just idle fantasies, rather than anything I had actually been up to with girls, but it did not come across that way, and my mother was disgusted. By the time I heard dad's key turn in the lock, I was shaking in my shoes.

"Look what your son has been up to," my mother sobbed, thrusting the offending diary into dad's hands. Sheila, to her credit, managed to keep the tears flowing for good measure. Dad took one look at the diary, grabbed me by the scruff of the neck and hollered, "GET UPSTAIRS, NOW!"

I took off, with dad in hot pursuit, but I did feel slightly surprised when he banged the flat of his hand against the wall as he ascended the stairs, making it sound as though he were giving me a beating. When we reached my bedroom, he let fly with a few more choice words about what a disgrace I was, then, surprisingly, placed half a crown in my hand and whispered,

"Don't ever keep a diary!"

I realised, at that moment, how much I loved him.

"You had better stay up here for a while until it all dies down," he concluded. I was happy to go along with that. Looking back now, I realise that was the first time dad treated me as an adult, and he was probably quite desperate for me to get on with the task of growing up.

STAYING THE COURSE

My departure from the world of childhood into pending adulthood meant that, first, I had to stay the course. I was fourteen and dad had finally seen fit to let me drive on quiet stretches of road, long before I had reached the legal driving age. Soon I was even allowed to drive his big lorry back to the depot in east London, with dad swearing at me the whole way. Dad considered teaching people to drive his speciality. Unfortunately, patience was not his strong point, and did not come so easily to him, so his lessons were punctuated with swear words, the occasional punch, and threats of what he would do if you crashed the gearbox one more time. I stuck with it and later, when it came to taking my driving test at the age of seventeen years and one month, I sailed through it as if I had been driving for years, which, of course, I had. My brother Sam also stayed the course with dad, and he, too, passed his test first time. However, my tough Uncle Terry and my sisters all gave up through sheer nerves and it took a few years before they got behind the wheel again. Uncle Terry, tough ex-sailor that he was, did not even have the bottle to tell dad that he did not want any more lessons. Instead, he got my mum to do it for him, saying, "I'd rather be an effing van boy all my life than suffer that abuse."

My budding adulthood exacerbated my fascination with the opposite sex. Brenda Smith lived opposite the school gates, in Longbridge Road, and by the time I was fifteen she was my steady girlfriend. Dad would have killed me had he known, but it didn't matter, I put an end to that little romance myself, through my own stupidity. Her parents had invited me around for tea and I duly turned up in my best suit with my hair immaculately styled into a fashionable "duck's arse". Their lovely spread was already on the table when there came a knock at the door.

"It's for you," a surprised Mrs Smith told me, ushering me out onto the porch. My mate Higgins stood there shuffling his feet and grinning.

"Terry," he whispered, "The boys are all going to Barking Baths. There's a dance on. They'll be birds everywhere!"

It was too good an opportunity to miss. Shamefully, I closed the front door behind me and cleared off to the dance, leaving a very angry Brenda and her bemused mum and dad wondering where on earth I had disappeared to. Brenda, understandably, refused to have anything to do with me after that, and I harboured deep remorse for years afterwards. Come to think of it, I would still like to say sorry. Despite our short liaison, I remember Brenda Smith and a few other girls more than I remember any of the lessons I took at school. As my school days drew to a close, I managed to get my name on the sheet for all nine subjects on my School Certificate – we did not have O and A levels back in those days. I had done well, but I still feel that I underachieved, I could have done better had I not been so distracted.

It was in my final school year that I had my first taste of business. It was an unmitigated disaster.

"Cotton, soaps, studs," the old lady called, as she dashed from house to house, with her crippled elderly husband limping along behind her, leaning on a pushcart stocked with the offered goods.

"Now, see that – that's the way to make a few quid, son," dad nodded appreciatively, convinced the old pair were making a fortune. He decided that we would establish a similar business on the Aveley council estate, trumping the "cotton woman" by using our Jowett Bradford van and extending the product range to vinegar, shampoo, soap powder and Vaseline. An electric bell, which, rather uselessly, was deafening to anyone inside but could hardly be heard outside the vehicle, was to herald our arrival. We crammed in the truck, surrounded by cartons of soap powder, shampoo, powder and a big barrel of a substance called "non-brewed condiment", which we were to pass off as malt vinegar, and set off for the first day's trading. Sam was to drive the van, we had decided, and mum, Sheila and myself would act as the sales staff. My dad, wisely, stayed at home ready to count the day's takings on our return. Having chosen a likely street to start trading, we nominated Sheila to knock on the first door, with the friendly sales line: "Any soap, soda, shampoo or vinegar?"

"Hello Sheila," the lady of the house greeted her, "fancy seeing you. Come in!" And with that Sheila disappeared for a cup of tea and did not emerge for about an hour. To make it worse, her friend did not even require any soap, soda, shampoo or vinegar. On account that Sheila was likely to be called in for tea at every house she called on, we decided to restrict her to the van while mum and I did the door knocking. I must have knocked on 100 doors without a single sale, and mum was doing no better over the other side of the road. Finally, I got a hit.

"How much is a sachet of Sunsilk shampoo?" the lady asked me.

"Sevenpence," came my triumphant reply.

"Ok, one sachet please," my generous customer answered. Down the path I ran, only to find that Sam had moved down the road rather quicker than I had and the van was nearly a mile away. I sprinted full speed to collect one sachet of shampoo, then sprinted all the way back to the lady to collect my sevenpence – and that was the total sum of our takings for the day! We jangled the bell to attract attention, but although it nearly burst our eardrums, it had no effect in drawing customers. When, in sheer frustration, mum threw open the window and yelled "Vin-e-gar" at the top of her lungs, my shy brother Sam quickly told her to shut up; it seemed he did not want to attract attention after all. At around 2 pm we decided to quit for the day and get some fish and chips, which resulted in a net loss of about two quid for that day. The business didn't last, but on the plus side mum didn't have to buy any soap, soda or vinegar for years afterwards. My first foray into the world of business gave no indication that years later I would go on to run or part-own many highly successful business ventures

THE LIFE OF A REPORTER

I lay on my bed idly, reading a Hank Jansen novel in which the journalist hero, typically for him, was bedding every girl he met. School was almost over and I had no idea what I wanted to do for a living, all I knew was that my part-time job selling newspapers outside Becontree Station was not going to keep me in the money for long. The life of a reporter, according to Hank Jansen, sounded pretty impressive, so when my classmate Bert Kellard told me he had applied for a position as a trainee reporter for the *Dagenham Post*, I decided to do likewise. I fired off a letter of application that was full of what you might call "journalistic licence" (and others may call embellished untruths), and was somewhat surprised when I was summoned for an interview with the group editor-in-chief of Greater London and Essex Newspapers, Mr Hugh Howton (I had no idea at the time that I would hold a similar post before I reached the age of 30). Sensibly, I got a proper haircut for the interview, dispensing with the duck's arse cut for a brand-new "college boy" look, expertly rendered by my brother Sam, who was now running his own salon in Lodge Avenue, Dagenham. I arrived in good time at 34 High Road, Ilford – a sorry-looking five-storey office building with the printing presses churning out behind it.

"Right this way, Mr, er, Hopley," Miss Cropley, the company's ancient accountant, who looked very much like our geography teacher and was just as fierce, showed me into the waiting room.

"Hopley!" Mr Howton burst into the waiting room, looking every inch the editor-in-chief, right down to the green sun shade he wore on his forehead. Multicoloured braces held up his loose-fitting trousers and silver arm bands kept his shirt sleeves from sliding down. He frantically waved a piece of copy paper, as if he hadn't a moment to spare.

"I've had nearly 50 applications for this position, son," he informed me once we had reached his office. "So what makes you think you should be considered for this role?"

"Well, sir, I can touch type, and, er," I cleared my throat nervously, knowing that I had to feed him the answers he wanted to hear, "I can write Pitman's shorthand".

"Yes," Mr Howton perused my letter of application as he spoke, "actually, that was the only reason you were selected for an interview and placed on the shortlist. Difficult field though, very difficult. Even my own son, Hugh Junior has applied."

My heart sank. I was left with the distinct impression I had no chance at all of getting this job. I fed him as much bullshit as I could during our half-hour interview and he was kind enough to give me a tour of the editorial department – they looked a right bunch of weirdos. Most had moved to London from the remoter parts of the UK, hoping for the opportunity to break into Fleet Street. They looked unlike any other young men I had encountered, with pipes stuck in their mouths and all wearing an expression of disdainful intelligence that was obviously beyond the comprehension of this cockney kid being introduced to them. Afterwards, I climbed on the number 23 bus, knowing that something special was needed to secure the job. Turns out, I was in luck. As the bus lumbered down the High Road, a brand-new car emerged from Jessup's showroom, accelerated across the road at right angles, and, with a screech and a crash, deposited itself in the window of the gents' outfitters opposite. Glass shattered across the street as the car continued to rev wildly in the window.

I was off that bus before it had stopped and at the scene, swinging immediately into big, important journalist mode. If I do say so myself, it was a very good story for a first effort. The poor old chap had just purchased a brand-new automatic car, assuring Peter Jessup, the car dealer, that he knew all about automatics. He had then put it into drive, put his foot down hard on the accelerator and turned the vehicle into a dangerous missile. The man was unhurt, but the car and the front window of the gents' outfitters were both complete write offs.

When I dived back into the newspaper office, demanding to speak to Mr Howton, I had names, addresses and a flowery description of the event at the ready. Hugh Howton appeared, looking exactly the same and still brandishing the piece of copy paper, probably the same piece.

"Mr Howton, I have my first story," I told him proudly, passing over the report I had scribbled down on the bus back to 34 High Road. The job was mine, although he did manage to find a vacancy for his son as well. I was to start in August 1954. First, however, there was enough time for a holiday – my first ever grown-up vacation without my mum and dad.

As a family we had taken family vacations in a chalet at Jaywick Sands, Essex, or a boarding house in Paignton, Devon, but this holiday was to be far removed from those tame family outings. George and Roy Dudley, Terry Higgins, Cloggy Clarke, Geoff Martin, David Hollington and myself were going on a boys' holiday away – a whole week at Warner's Holiday Camp. There was to be plenty of booze, and even more crumpet. Better yet, we had decided that the best way to get there was to hire a car, and the fact that none of us had our licence as of yet was no deterrent. I simply "borrowed" my brother's licence and worked on fraudulently recreating his signature. For good measure I also borrowed a couple of his suits, hoping he wouldn't notice (he did, of course, and gave me a hiding for it afterwards). The car we hired was a Morris Minor, not the ideal choice for seven beefy teenage boys, particularly after the 1000cc car was made a little shorter by someone hitting us up the rear just a few miles after we left home. But not even that could dampen our spirits. We were seven teenagers let loose for the first time and we planned to make the most of our newfound freedom.

As we soothed our hung-over heads the morning after our first night at Warner's, it came as quite a surprise to hear a tap on the door. It was the manager, summoning us to his office to explain our behaviour the night before.

"Climbing on stage and drunkenly singing with the band, out of tune I might add, is no way to conduct yourself on your first night at Warner's Holiday Camp, boys," he growled sternly. "This is a holiday establishment. People are here to have fun, but within reason. Give me one good reason why I shouldn't turn you all out this instance?" He fixed me with a level stare.

"Sorry, we didn't know singing was forbidden," I cheekily countered, doing my best to feign an innocent expression. The manager sighed in exasperation and I quickly followed on with, "Really, the lads and I are just here to have a good time. It was our first night, you know, and we don't intend to make any trouble. It's just that there are seven of us and, well, we're all healthy lads you know. We promise not to be unruly but I really don't think some of the lads would take too kindly to you banning us from the camp after we've made a promise to be on our best behaviour. D'you know what I mean?" I added the thinly veiled threat, working my powers of persuasion to the hilt.

The manager, knowing that he was probably better off to ignore the first night shenanigans, gave us the benefit of the doubt. From then on, we were on our best behaviour – almost. We still drank too much most nights and determinedly attempted to further our sex education, with the help of two sisters from Sheffield.

"I'm going to give Quatie Quatie a treat tonight," Higgins informed us as he checked his unruly hair in the mirror. He was referring to one of the sisters, Katie, who was nicknamed Quatie thanks to her unfortunate speech impediment. Higgins was always a bit of a ladies man and was convinced young Katie would go for him big time. Both George and I didn't shatter the illusion by telling him we had already made her acquaintance.

"You tell me, Higgins, you're the movie star," I joked. I could write a whole book on Higgins – but, you see, others already have. He was the only one of us who had not yet landed a job by the time we took our holiday and there was much mirth about his proposed career prospects. He had been holding out because he wanted to be a film star, of all things.

"Whatever happens," one of the other lads added, "If you get lucky don't tell them where you live."

"Why's that? What if they want to come to visit?" Dave Hollington enquired innocently.

"Because, I don't know about you, but I'm not quite ready to be a father just yet," I added with a wink. I am ashamed that not telling them where we lived was our version of safe sex, but it was typical mentality at that time, and we were lads still on the cusp of manhood. We wanted to enjoy the benefits without the responsibility. Thankfully, it never came to that, but Geoff Martin, who as far as I know had nothing to be worried about anyway, did receive a thick ear from Higgins when he was overheard explaining to the two sisters from Sheffield, "You come out of Becontree Station, turn right, go down the steps and that's our road."

I later learned in life that sometimes even the most unlikely dreams come true and it was not long after our holiday that Higgins did indeed became famous. He enjoyed a whirlwind romance with a very attractive American girl named Sandie, whom he had met at Tottenham Royal. Obviously not heeding the warning of our earlier pact, he soon accidentally put her in the family way. Not only was she very attractive, she also happened to have very wealthy parents. In no time at all they were married and Higgins became a man about town in his new Mercedes 300 gull-wing sports car, which had been a wedding present to him from his new father-in-law. Deciding that the name Higgins was too "common", he promptly changed it and faded from our social scene. The next time we saw him was on our TV screen fighting with Patrick McGoohan in Dangerman. Neither the acting gig nor the marriage were to last, but the new surname did. Terry de Havilland became a flamboyant shoe designer and was world renowned as the "Cobbler to the Stars". Television programmes have been made about his life and books published and, although I haven't seen him from that day to this, I wonder whether Jackie Kennedy would still have bought his shoes if she'd known he was really just good old Terry Higgins from Essex.

THE PATH TO SUCCESS

I started my journalistic career in August 1954 – the same day as Hugh Howton Junior, the boss's son. By pure coincidence, I immediately made an impact by stumbling across the biggest story the Dagenham Post had run in years. As my bus lumbered along Whalebone Lane one morning, a very attractive young lady wearing a short skirt and stilettos caught my attention as she hopped into the passenger seat of a car. Not so amazing you might think, but that same evening as my bus passed the spot I saw the same woman again, stepping into another car. The following day, a different girl, also attired in a diminutive skirt and high heels, clambered into another car. It took a few days before the penny dropped – a team of prostitutes was operating right in the middle of working class Dagenham! In true investigative journalism style, I told no one, keeping my eyes open for more evidence. Sure enough, I was right – Whalebone Lane was full of kerb crawlers in the evenings and several 'ladies of the night' were offering their services. The story I wrote on the scandal got me my first coveted by-line. The next day, my little exposé was all over the national press. Such goings on were unheard of in suburbia in the fifties, so I was very proud to be the reporter who broke the story.

"Terry, there's an, er, lady, here to see you," the receptionist informed me a few days later.

"Really?" I asked, confused, "I don't recall making any appointments." Perplexed as to why a young lady would be visiting me at work, I followed the receptionist back out to the foyer. My heart sank as I saw a not-so-young, heavily made up blonde who could only have been one thing – one of the streetwalkers I had recently exposed.

"Mr Hopley?" she asked, and I nodded, expecting her to launch into a tirade of abuse at any moment.

"I've come to thank you, personally," she slurred the last word lasciviously. "Since you ran that story, business has trebled. I can't thank you enough for bringing Whalebone Lane to everyone's attention. In fact, if there is anything I can do to repay you, anything at all, you know where to find me."

I blushed. It was blatantly and embarrassingly apparent that she was offering to show her gratitude with a season ticket.

"Er, no, er, thanks all the same," I blustered, giving a slight chuckle as my newfound admirer departed the office. Thanks to my story, Whalebone Lane rose from the ranks of erstwhile pickup place to full-blown red light district in its own right. It was a couple of years before the police managed to drive the girls elsewhere.

I enjoyed my job and thrived on ambition, and within months I had been promoted to writing a weekly page on films and show business, which might mean anything from attending the local drama group's amateur production to the occasional trip to the West End to attend a film premiere or show. It was a highly sought after gig, thanks to the perks of free admission to London cinemas and theatres. While attending the press show of Doctor at Sea, I sat next to (and successfully managed to chat up) a beautiful doe-eyed blonde better known as Brigitte Bardot – just one of the fringe benefits. Brigitte, like me, was new to her business and we struck up quite a rapport during lunch. How close did we get? Book or no book that is a secret I am not prepared to share.

As a result of my "show business" reporting, I even made a bit of a name for myself at Ilford Palais when a flamboyant new manager named Jimmy Savile came on the scene. Jimmy had peroxide-blond hair, drove a Jaguar XK120 and was a tireless self-promoter who expertly garnered a large share of publicity in the local press – all hallmarks of extroversion that led to his later success as a TV personality. Savile ran a weekly contest to entice local girls to the Palais: one week a beauty contest, one week a jive competition and the next week a "sweater girl" contest. By some masterstroke of luck, I was nominated as the sole judge, which made me quite popular with the girls. Looking back now I can spot a sordid side to his personality but at the time it all seemed such harmless fun. For instance, I remember choosing the three finalists for a sweater-girl competition when Savile informed them they would have to be checked by me personally to make sure they were not wearing falsies

"Off you go, enjoy yourself," he whispered to me, but I didn't have the bottle.

Show-business perks were even enough for me to score lunch (but only lunch, unfortunately) with Petula Clark following a radio show called Workers Playtime. As is the intricate web of life, it was actually attending that event that led to my gradual transition from general reporter to rising sports journalist. The radio show was broadcast from the canteen of a sports ground owned by enterprising local company Dagenham Cables, and it was at this sports ground that I was to meet a boy who remains one of my closest mates. At the time, this fresh-faced local kid called Geoff Hurst was playing cricket for the Essex Club and Ground team, trying to make up his mind whether to be a professional cricketer or footballer. Every football fan in England is grateful he chose football! Even now, nearly 50 years later, his fame as a player for West Ham and England and the memory of his hat-trick on that magical day in 1966 when England beat Germany 4–2 to take home that most coveted of all sporting trophies, is engraved on every football lover's mind. I harboured a desire to become a sports reporter and Geoff's friendship was instrumental in helping me achieve that goal. In fact his friendship became, and still is, a part of my life and that of my family that we truly cherish. When, in 1998, he was knighted by the Queen for his services to football I was proud when he announced he wanted only one speaker at the official reception…me!

Meanwhile, my reporting career was coming along in leaps and bounds, what with the show-business page and a one-day-a-week court reporting job, which was nothing if not informative. I was just an impressionable seventeen-year-old and had never really conceived of the idea of a 'flasher' until my first day on the Press Bench at the Stratford Magistrates Court. I sat quietly and made notes of the proceedings, not expecting to get a laugh out of the case. Standing in the dock was a middle-aged man (who incidentally also looked remarkably like one of my former teachers, but wasn't) who had been charged with indecent exposure. The witness, a teenage girl who to my inexperienced eye looked like she had been around a fair bit herself, was being questioned by the prosecution about the man's alleged flashing. His defence had been that he was merely relieving himself when the girl had chanced by and had peered at him. She maintained that he had flashed her in the traditional way by opening his Macintosh. The prosecution knew that if they could prove the man had an erection, it would reveal a sexual motive for his exposure, which would aid their case, but asking the girl directly would have been a leading question that the judge would have disallowed. Somehow, the prosecutor had to get the girl to say he had an erection without asking her the question outright.

"So," the prosecutor reasoned, "you have already told the court you clearly saw this man's penis. In what condition was it?"

"Oh it was in very good condition," the young witness added, quick as a flash, sending the court into uproar. Court reporting, it seemed on my first day, was quite a laugh. However, I soon found out that more often than not it involved simply filling notebooks with the mundane outcomes of motoring offences and domestic disputes. And unfortunately, neither of the two memorable cases I covered made it into print because they were considered a bit ribald for our readers. Another humorous piece of evidence-giving was again due to the prosecution instructing their witness in the ways to avoid a judge interjecting and dismissing testimony. A young girl had been called to the stand to describe her molestation at the hands of an older man. She had clearly been carefully briefed by the prosecuting counsel as to how she should describe the molestation.

"He put his hand up my dress…" she began, throwing a fleeting, shy glance at the prosecutor for approval. "…then he touched my…" she paused, for what seemed an age, then turned to the prosecutor and asked, "Hey mister, what's that word you told me to use for my fanny?"

Both men were found guilty but neither of these incidents were suitable for publication at the time. Along with court reporting, I also attended County Council meetings, which were usually dull affairs punctuated with occasional heated discussions and witty remarks from some of the very blunt Essex farmers. I recall one meeting where a droll fellow, arguing that the hose and pump on an ancient fire engine in his village required replacing, stood up and interjected: "Mr Chairman, I could piss further than that fire engine!"

"Sit down, Sir, you are out of order," the chairman rebuked.

"I would be out of order if I couldn't piss further than that fire engine!" came the farmer's rebuttal.

I was aided in my journalistic forays by a baby-faced blond kid on the editorial team – John Bromley. John was not only a talented writer, he was also a laugh a minute, and we got in and out of quite a few scrapes together. John set his star on moving into radio or television and together we got a part-time job with Radio Luxembourg. It was London's first pirate radio station and our programme was sponsored by Lyons confectionery, so we decided to start a promotion whereby we would randomly call dozens of phone numbers and anyone who answered the phone with the words "Lyons Mint Chocs" would receive a handsome hamper of goodies. The idea was to inspire people to answer the phone "Lyons Mint Chocs" but, of course, at first no one ever did. John and I spent fruitless hours on the phone in the vain hope that just one person might say the magic words, then, eventually, we moved to less labour-intensive methods. Rather than ringing random numbers, we began phoning our friends, who had been pre-warned. This not only increased our standing with our sponsor, Lyons, it also increased our popularity in our social set as our mates began to reap the benefits.

At around the same time, the *Daily Express* was running a "Knights of the Road" club in which "good driving ambassadors" reported to the paper the registration numbers of courteous drivers. The paper then published the numbers, entitling the registration holder to a five pound prize. Of course, five quid was a lot of money in the fifties, so, with a bit of clever wangling, John and I got ourselves appointed good driving ambassadors and our friends duly collected their membership badges and 50 per cent of the prize money. The other 50 per cent lined our entrepreneurial pockets. With such a go-getting attitude, John Bromley did, of course, make it into television, rising to become the head of ITV Sport before he died tragically at an early age.

Another young reporter in my office was one of life's great characters. Rodney Bennett-England had sprung from a modest semi-detached house in Romford, Essex, but put on all the airs and graces of a blue-blood. He was usually decked out as a true dandy, wearing a navy blue overcoat complete with velvet collar set off by a bowler hat. Rodney had managed to score the plum job of motoring correspondent, which entailed test-driving the latest flash set of wheels on the market, adding to his debonair image. Unfortunately, while his position provided the grand car, it did not pay all that well, so Rodney seldom had the funds to put petrol in! When the manufacturers came to collect their test car, Rodney would ensure he left no more than a thimbleful of fuel in it for them to get to the nearest garage. On one occasion, he and I had a big impressive Daimler to road test. When it was due to be picked up, the petrol gauge was showing just below empty. Suddenly, the call came through that there was a big fire and Rodney and I were dispatched to cover it, but, since I didn't have my own transport, we had no choice but to take the Daimler. I can still see the face of the petrol pump attendant (no self-service pumps back in those days, of course) when Rodney drove up, complete with velvet collar and bowler hat, and requested, "Half a gallon, please."

"Blimey! Where are you going, mate, Scotland?" came the attendant's reply.

LOVE AND LOSS

I enjoyed my work, whether covering a sedate local flower show or dining with the stars in the West End, but while the lifestyle of a trainee journalist was a lot of fun, it had to be lived on minimal funds. I managed, until the worst years of my life sprang upon me. Dad's illness, like most life-changing events, came as a complete surprise. Dad was in his mid-forties and had been complaining of stomach pains for a few years, but even that did not hint at the shock that lay ahead. Mum had taken him to London Hospital, where he had been diagnosed with a duodenal ulcer and was to have what was considered fairly routine surgery to have it removed. When mum and I visited him after the operation, dad was sitting up in bed, smiling broadly and feeling better. Like most men of the age, he was not the kind to take too happily to being in hospital.

"I don't think I'll be in here too long," he told mum optimistically. "Hop down to the sister's office, Terry, and ask when I can get out of here," he instructed. I made my way to the sister's office, which had a large window overlooking the ward. I could still see mum and dad chatting and laughing as I poked my head in, looking for the sister. She was not there, but a young doctor sat behind the desk.

"Excuse me," I gestured towards dad through the glass, "any chance of my dad going home today?"

The doctor's reply remains indelible in my mind.

"How old are you?" he queried.

"Seventeen."

"Sit down," he instructed.

I sat. I could still see dad watching through the window.

"Your dad has cancer. He is going to die. There is nothing we can do. He can go home whenever you like. We just opened him up and stitched him back up again. There is absolutely nothing we can do to help him."

I was in complete shock. How could he break that news to me, a seventeen-year-old kid, just like that? Had he made a mistake? It just could not be true. But it was. I would like to think that I inherited some of my father's stoicism, and it was that stoicism that forced a smile on my face as I made my way back to the ward.

"The doctor said you can come home, dad," I told my father, doing my level best to keep the doctor's grim news from showing on my face. "He said everything is ok but you might get a bit more pain before you get better." It was the best I could do. It seems inconceivable nowadays, but there was no way that I could relay that terrible news to my family, it would break their hearts and my dad's spirit. Just the word 'cancer' hit with all the effect of a sledgehammer. In the fifties, there was little treatment available and dad's diagnosis was considered pretty much a death sentence. I was distraught. I could tell no one. While I suffered through sleepless nights, mum, dad and my siblings were full of the joys of spring, believing the operation was a big success. I alone knew the truth and struggled with my choices. What should I do? What could I do? Who should I tell? Should I bear this knowledge alone?

For days I kept that gut-wrenching secret, but eventually I had to tell my older brother, Sam. Sharing that unbearable knowledge brought the two of us closer than we had probably ever been. We sobbed our hearts out together, deciding whether to tell the others. The next day, we told Jessie and Sheila and the four of us shared the burden for several months until dad's visible deterioration, both physically and mentally, made it impossible for us to keep the diagnosis from mum. We decided it would only cause dad pain to know that the operation had been a complete sham, so my father never knew the truth. Keeping the knowledge of his illness from my masculine, protective father was considered an act of kindness, although it is not how things would have been done nowadays. Dad was a man of few words and there were few words we could have said that would have made those long months of his illness any better. I pleaded with our GP for help, and, when my pleas were ignored, I threatened, but it was to no avail. There was, they assured me, nothing they could do in the face of dad's terrible illness. Dad's pain was visceral and prolonged, but it seemed no one in the medical profession wanted to know. We watched helplessly, as our once 14-stone superman became a palliative skeleton, dejected and in pain. All of my family moved back home as the end approached (even the girls, who were by now married) and we took solace in each other's company. The four of us were devastated, and only my mother remained strong. I am sure her strength has granted her a place as a saint. Each night, she sat up with dad in his agony, cradling his head in her lap. It was only once my father was nearing the end of that long, lonely corridor, that morphine turned his lurking shadows into a hazy twilight glow. Before he died, dad took each of us aside and, in a quiet voice, said those sad, touching, personal things he wanted to say before he went.

"I always had big plans for you, Terry," he told me, as I fought hard to swallow the lump in my throat. "Not being there to guide you…to help you achieve them is…well, it's terrifying, son," he added, his voice choked with emotion.

"Take care of your mother and your sisters for me. And if you have a problem to sort out, use your brain. If you have a troublemaker to sort out, use Uncle Terry."

Dad had guided me brilliantly for seventeen years. Now that I am well past the age my father was when he died, I hope one day I can sit with him again and he can be proud of the things that went right, and laugh with me at the things that went wrong.

PROVIDING

One of the things that definitely went wrong was my hasty departure from the role of trainee journalist soon after my dad's passing. Living on a small salary of just three pounds a week had been acceptable for a single youth, but now I had a family to support. Losing dad left a gaping hole in our lives, one that Sam and I, as the next generation of Hopley men, were determined to try to fill, as futile as it was to think we could ever compensate for the loss of such a man. I was not to be the only one of my friends to be so suddenly thrust into the world of the provider. Within weeks, George and Roy's dad also succumbed to the dreaded cancer and those carefree boys who had enjoyed that irresponsible holiday at Warner's Camp were well and truly men. I meant to provide for mum as best I could, and that meant committing an unforgivable sin – asking for a pay rise.

"You may be aware that recently…" I caught my breath as I looked across at Mrs Ruby Browning, the kindly company chairman who had inherited the business on the death of her own father, "…my father recently passed away. And it is very difficult to support my mother on my salary. Please, Mrs Browning, I wondered whether I might have a salary increase?"

Mrs Browning was a lovely, sympathetic woman and reassured me that, indeed, she was sure this was possible but she would have to run it by her husband, Clarence, who was also a director. Unfortunately, Clarence proved far less sympathetic.

"The board has carefully considered your application for an increase and regret that nothing can be done," he looked down at the desk to avoid eye contact with me. I stared at him incredulously, my face murderous at hearing his news.

"If we give you more money, we would have to do the same for all of our trainees," he added weakly, further increasing my ire. What he said next really tipped me over the edge.

"Tell your mother to get a job."

From that moment, I decided I was finished with the newspaper.

"She will not be getting a job," I answered firmly, "But I will be getting a new job. I quit! Take this conversation as my resignation. I will finish up by the week's end," and with that, I stood up and turned to leave. Mr Browning looked stunned. It was clear he had not anticipated this.

"You can't just quit," he remonstrated. "You signed apprenticeship papers that prevent it. You are not allowed to leave!"

"Watch me!" I spat, as I stalked out the door.

My career as a journalist was over, or so I thought. Now I had to set about earning some real money. Unfortunately, real work wasn't quite as easy as I had anticipated. Baker, tailor shop assistant, stonemason – I tried just about anything but nothing quite delivered what it promised. The bakery had sounded like a dream come true. All I had to do was unload bread from the ovens for twenty minutes and then enjoy a forty-minute spell while the next batch of loaves were baking. I quickly found out that as soon as the oven doors opened, that twenty-minute stint of work was carried out at temperatures so high you felt as if you were in the oven yourself. Another drawback was that the scorching hot loaves had to be carried from the conveyor belt to the trolleys with my bare hands. The heat was intolerable and at the end of my first day, with my face baked to a reddish sheen and blisters all over my hands, I was sacked for retreating to the cool of the yard when I should have been steaming my body some more and standing by the ovens. I cannot say I was devastated that job was over.

My time as a tailor was no better. My Jewish boss expected me to work eighteen-hour days for a pittance more than I earned as a trainee journalist. I moved on to the stonemasons, where George Dudley had told me he earned good money lugging big lumps of stone around.

"Here you go," the boss instructed, handing me a shovel and pointing towards a sizable stack of stone chippings, "shovel those onto the back of the lorry for me."

Eager to impress, I immediately bent down to take my first shovelful when the unlucky sound of cloth tearing alerted me to the fact that my trousers had split down the middle seam! You can imagine how much ribbing I received from all of the other labourers as I toiled away all day with my backside hanging out, exposed to the elements and the ridicule of my colleagues. I fared little better on my second day, which was also to be my last day as a would-be stonemason. I was instructed to stand on top of a large chunk of stone to shovel a substance called shot into the cut being made by a giant saw. It appeared to me that as fast as I shovelled the shot, the blade of the saw simply ground it out again, which seemed rather pointless. So I decided not to bother shovelling, which had dire consequences. Suddenly, the cut went off at an odd angle and the very expensive blade was totally destroyed. The boss and I mutually decided that stonemasonry really was not the career for me. With three failed positions under my belt, I decided to keep it simple and stick to a career already in the family. My brother Sam was successfully running his own hairdressers, and Sheila, who traditionally had as much luck with jobs as I was now experiencing, had joined him. Time to add another family member to the barbershop trade, I thought. I would become a hairdresser.

NATIONAL SERVICE

I would return to hairdressing on a few occasions in my life, and even part-own a salon at one point, but it was certainly always a stop-gap solution. Something else always came up to relieve me of my hair-cutting duties, which I am sure Sam was grateful for (I usually was too). This time, however, it was to be an interesting and unexpected turn of events, and one that would require me to have a haircut!

As the clippers buzzed over my head, removing every last skerrick of my stylish "college boy" hairdo in favour of a harsh short back and sides, I pondered once again why on earth I had quit journalism. In throwing in the towel, I had made one fatal oversight. While employed as a trainee journalist I was temporarily excused national service, but as soon as I quit the army caught up with me. I was quickly packed up and on a train to Aldershot, where I was to undergo two months in the training battalion of the Royal Army Service Corps. I passed the medical with flying colours and, after my first day's induction, prepared for my first bleak night in the barracks. The barracks consisted of Mizzen huts with one or two storeys, each of which housed a number of men of varying degrees of strength and temperament. Like most new recruits, I struggled to come to terms with suddenly sharing my bedroom with other men and being so far from the familiarity of friends and family. I was surrounded by other soldiers, but there was not that instant feeling of camaraderie you expect from men placed in that position. Most of the new recruits withdrew to their own beds to try to comprehend what they could expect tomorrow, and those that had already been in the army a few weeks were indifferent to the newcomers or swaggered around bullying the easiest picks of the recruits. Even for me, knowing I could hold my own, that first night was extremely long and lonely. After laying out my kit in preparation for training the next morning, I slumped on my bed, rubbed my newly bald head in consternation, and tried to anticipate what the morning would bring before I drifted into a fitful sleep.

"Effing new recruits," I awoke with a jolt, hitting the floor hard as the taunting, face of a north country boy leered down at me. "How'd you like that then?" he jeered, but not for long, because in one movement I sprang up from the bed and whacked him as hard as I could right on the point of the jaw. He hit the deck with an immediacy that would have made Uncle Terry proud. It was then that I noticed that not only had he tipped me out of bed, he had kicked my freshly laid-out kit across the floor of the hut. In retaliation, while he crawled to his knees trying to work out who he was and where he was, I marched over to his bed, threw his meagre personal possessions on his slim mattress, rolled it up like a kit and hurled it out of the second-storey window into the pouring rain.

'How'd you like that then?' I retorted, as I gave him a dose of his own medicine, to the admiring glances of some of the more retiring boys who had already been on the receiving end of his bullying. For the entire two months of training, bullying remained rife, but this act saved me from being a target. Smaller, less able boys copped the brunt of the attacks and even within my first week I saw young soldiers reduced to tears. In those days, although it was often hushed up, it was not uncommon for servicemen to commit suicide. I became a bit of a hero to some of the more sensitive young soldiers and intervened where I could to stop them being targeted.

The training itself seemed to suit me and after the first rude shock of army life, I even began to enjoy the 5am endurance runs and assault courses. I was pretty fit and even more confident, and was rarely fooled by the overbearing bravado of the non-commissioned officers. They shouted orders and made threats in typical army style, but on the whole they were scathing only of those who were physically not up to army life – so the weaker boys copped a bollocking on the running track as well as in the barracks. Despite enjoying challenging my body physically, I did not always enjoy the way of life. The food was unlike anything I had encountered before and gave new meaning to the term 'mess tin'. Great globs of a questionable colour and flavour were ladled into each mess tin daily, varying only slightly in consistency and taste. Sometimes we could distinguish from which vegetable or animal the food was derived, but more often than not it remained a mystery. Still, it was edible and we had to fuel the daily exercise somehow, so we ate it without too much comment. Most of all, I missed my privacy and my family.

"What you do," one of the young soldiers in my barracks informed me, "is report yourself sick on a Thursday night, because the medical officer's off at lunchtime on a Friday and he's gone for the entire weekend. So you're not really sick and you can clear off for the weekend, head back home and then make sure you're back before Monday morning when the med officer signs back in," he nodded sagely. It sounded like a great plan to me and I resolved to try it.

"I'm really not feeling well, sir." I clutched my stomach feebly in the best impression of a man struck down with virulence. "Think I better spend a few days in the sick bay." My plan worked a treat. I was admitted to the sick bay Thursday night and was glad to find that it was inhabited by just two others, both of whom were actually sick, making them unlikely to care about, or notice, my disappearing act the following day. Unfortunately, the fact that they were really sick was to be my downfall. By the time the medical officer left at twelve o'clock Friday, my faux sickness had developed into real symptoms. By Friday afternoon, I was not just feeling sick, I had a very high temperature and was transferred to hospital that night. My little weekend holiday turned into a week in hospital, subsisting on hospital food that was only marginally better than the slop served in the mess hall. Hardly a master plan after all! However, my wish for privacy was granted.

Because each block of training lasted two weeks (for example two weeks of physical fitness training followed by two weeks of munitions training) when I returned to the barracks, north country boy and the rest of my intake had moved on. As the new intake for the rifle training course was yet to arrive, I found myself the sole occupant of my billet for a week or so while I waited for the next intake of recruits. Of course, at first I was pretty pleased about this development, but that night, when the lights went out in my cold, empty Mizzen hut, which stood alone in the centre of a field, the scurrying of tiny feet and the gnawing noises in the walls alerted me to the fact that I was not alone after all. I was surrounded by a battalion of rats! That night, I would have given almost anything not to have my privacy.

My months of training passed quickly and I was one of the lucky ones for whom it all came relatively easily. As the day of our passing out parade grew near, I was proud to learn that my hard work had paid off – out of all the men I had trained with, I had been chosen as champion recruit of the battalion. Mum and Sheila, who came to watch the parade, were immensely proud as I stood out from the khaki-clad ranks in my special white gaiters and belt, beaming as the commanding officer presented me with my medal. I still have the medal today. Little did I know, but being in uniform suited me; later in life, it would continue to be a sign of my standing, albeit at sea, rather than on land.

Being chosen as the champion recruit opened up doors I had never even conceived of until then. I was called to an interview with the War Office Selection Board. Thankfully, I was shrewd enough to play them at their own game. They wanted me to do officer training and sign on as a regular soldier; I wanted an opportunity to rise above the rank and file. It was a win-win situation. I polished up my cockney accent, put a few inspired trimmings on my educational record and convinced them that my father was the director of a transport company, rather than a humble lorry driver, and I was on my way to a special role in military intelligence. It meant signing up for a further six-month term, but promised a fantastic choice of postings.

"You have a number of options," I was told by the recruitment officer of SHAPE (Supreme Headquarters of Allied Powers of Europe). "An attachment to our embassy in Washington, USA; a military intelligence role at SHAPE headquarters in Fontainbleu, France; or a move to the Admiralty Building in Whitehall…"

The range of opportunities left me stunned, but I knew which one would suit me best. I'd had it with earning a pittance, and I knew that the position with the MoD in Whitehall came with an impressive number of allowances. It also meant I could live at home with mum and wouldn't have to wear a uniform. All of a sudden, I found myself helping run the country's defence from the very comfortable surrounds of the War Office, the Admiralty, and my own bedroom.

THE LITTLE GIRL I FELL FOR

It also meant I was back to chasing the girls at Cambell Youth Club with George and Roy Dudley, and it was there that one of the definite "things that went right" in my life occurred. It came in the shape of Jean Flavin – a petite fifteen-year-old with a mass of tight, springy curls, beautiful blue eyes and a shy smile that stopped me in my tracks. Of course, the path to true love is rarely smooth and there were a few glitches in the early days of our courtship, not the least Roy Dudley. His older brother George had already been hit by Cupid's arrow and had fallen for fourteen-year-old Mavis Young – still a wonderful friend, who was instrumental in my business success years later – and I think that made Roy also keen to get himself some romantic action. At the time, I was busy being as flash and confident as possible (and why not, I was an officer with a great position in military intelligence – if I couldn't use that to impress the girls, then what was I doing?) and fancied myself as a bit of a jiver. The first time Jean saw me, I was busy showing off and jiving with Josephine Tarrant in front of a large, cheering crowd at the youth club. Jean later admitted that the only thing she liked about me that night was my Donegal tweed suit! Meanwhile, I liked the challenge of convincing such a reticent girl to like me, and I think that was part of the attraction, but I was not always so sure about Jean's lovely curly hair. I remember thinking that she'd had a perm that had gone wrong! Roy Dudley, it seemed, also had a soft spot for this quietly spoken young beauty. Roy was a lot less cocky than I was, but he had mustered up the courage to take Jean to a dance. She was an excellent dancer, with fabulous legs to match, and had appeared on several television shows, including The Benny Hill Show, Crackerjack and the Billy Cotton Band Show. Unfortunately for Roy, he took Jean to the dance, but I took her home, since I was far more forward in these matters than him. The rest, as they say, is history – a history of more than 50 years of wedded bliss for my lovely wife and me, but some things never change. Jean still stops me in my tracks and she still has lovely legs. Not only that,she can put on a pair of tap shoes and show the grandchildren and great grandchildren how it is done.

Luckily, Roy forgave me and he and I bought our first car together soon after. We borrowed twenty-five pounds from a Christmas loan club, which we had to pay back at half a crown a week, and bought a 1934 Standard 12 Saloon with a running board, a blind in the back window and a starting handle to crank the engine into life. Roy wanted it to look like the new Ford Zodiac, so we painted it red and black and even white-walled the tyres, which were run down to the canvas. Some of my fondest memories of courting Jean took place in the backseat of that car, with the blind down. When we finally sold it, after about a year, we got fifty quid for it – double what we paid – and I immediately blew the lot on clothes. Roy soon found true love when he met and married Mary Cox, who lived next door to Dudley Moore. Remember those brilliant sketches Dudley Moore performed with Peter Cook? Well all of the names mentioned in them were actually neighbours and it was quite a laugh waiting to see who would get a mention next:

Dear Miss Flavin,
Due to the threat of nuclear conflict, the British Government has decided that an air raid warden should be appointed for every road in the country. You have been selected as the air raid warden for your road. You are required to attend a weekly training session at Dagenham Civic Centre at 1930hrs every Monday, starting next week. You are required to wear the following: Wellington Boots, a plastic Mac and a tin helmet. Please bring with you two household buckets filled with sand, a 50-foot length of hosepipe and a pickaxe.
Yours sincerely,
The British War Office

Another of Jean's great qualities is her sense of humour, and, no stranger to practical jokes myself, I took it upon myself to use my position (and sometimes the office's letterhead) to my best advantage. Of course, I never used it for anything that could be problematic but it was handy to have envelopes emblazoned with "On Her Majesty's Service" at my disposal. Mind you, when I arrived at the council house Jean shared with her mum, dad and sister Carol the day after sending the letter, I discovered Jean was rather more gullible than I had expected.

"How is Jean going to carry all that equipment on a bus?" sobbed her mother, "I'm going to have to write to them and tell them to find someone stronger to be the air raid warden," she threatened.

I bit back a laugh and considered not even telling them it was a joke, if only to see my welly-wearing five-foot-nothing girlfriend trying to carry two buckets of sand onto a bus, but thought better of it. I couldn't be that cruel.

"Didn't the fact that I work at the British War Office give you a clue?" I later laughed, but neither Jean nor her mum found it particularly funny. It was months before they forgave me and Jean still brings it up occasionally – half a century later.

FUN AND GAMES

It was not all fun and games at the War Office, sometimes we actually did some work. I worked in naval intelligence, but I cannot tell you what we did, because then I would have to kill you. However, there were still a few conflicts bubbling away around the world and my journalistic skills were sometimes employed to construct signals to overseas units. Of course, while we composed the signals, we did not actually send them; that task fell to the Military Operations Unit next door. On occasion I was also called up for night duty at the War Office, which mostly consisted of sitting there reading the Beano until about midnight, upon which I retired to a nice little room with quite a comfortable bed. One time on night duty, I had constructed a signal that I felt slightly nervous about sending because it had not been checked by anyone in my department (the senior duty intelligence office having retired to his club for a few hours – as I said, it was not all fun and games, but it certainly was not all work either). I knew it had to pass through Military Operations anyway and I felt reasonably confident that they would obviously spot it if I was accidentally starting World War III, but just to be sure I took the signal personally to the duty officer in Military Operations, whom I had not yet met.

I respectfully knocked on the door and was greeted with a very public-school voice saying, "Come in."

Pushing open the door, my jaw hit the floor when I saw who sat behind the desk.

"What on earth are you doing here?" Rodney Bennett-England and I chorused in unison, each pointing at the other. Here we were, two ex-trainee reporters running the defence of the United Kingdom between us!

Another time on night duty, I was interrupted in my reading by the entrance of an unobtrusive looking man in a slightly crumpled navy blue suit.

"What do you want?" I asked rather brusquely, thinking he was a messenger.

"I am the chief of the Imperial General Staff," he replied, fixing me with a gaze, "Where is Major Llewellyn?"

Thinking it was a gag, I was just about to reply "And I am admiral of the fleet" when I thought better of it, after all discretion was the better part of valour. This meant I had some quick thinking to do because, as usual, Major Llewellyn had disappeared to his club when he really shouldn't have. Fortunately, I tracked down his phone number and panted down the line, "There's some guy here reckons he's Field Marshal Sir Gerald Templar." Major Llewellyn was back so quickly the field marshal was hardly kept waiting.

I loved my job. It came with many benefits, not least of which was a civilian clothing allowance, a travel allowance, a living at home allowance and a ration allowance. It also was not so demanding that I couldn't squeeze in a few extracurricular activities. Jean would catch the tube down from her job in an insurance office at Monument, and she and I would spend a few hours each day dancing at the Lyceum ballroom in The Strand over my lunch break. I also attended the Morris School of Hairdressing and practised on my compatriots in an underground room at the Admiralty, which really should have been set aside in case of a nuclear attack, but since that seemed entirely unlikely at the time, it made a perfect salon.

A CUT ABOVE

My work in the underground salon proved worthwhile, because it was not to be long before I was back to hairdressing. It had nothing to do with my somewhat lax approach to work at the Admiralty (that seemed to be a pre-requisite for the staff there) because before my scheduled demob I was called in by the top brass and offered the chance to become a regular officer. I turned it down. The job security and the perks were tempting, but Jean and I had discussed it at length and it seemed so far removed from our working-class upbringing that I just couldn't see myself doing it. When the time came for my demob, I went back to work for my brother in his barbershop in Lodge Avenue, Dagenham – for no reason than that I could not think of anything else to do! As I stood there each day, bored with giving trims, short back-and-sides and crewcuts, I dreamed of marrying Jean and finding a job as a sales representative. I even made the token effort of applying for a job as a pet food sales representative (funnily enough, that was the only job interview I ever failed). Sam's hairdressing business was doing well, and he needed more staff, so he dispatched me to the office of the Dagenham Post (my old stomping ground) to hand in a classified advertisement for staff.

"Terry Hopley," Bob Hutchins, the editor, accosted me in the reception area, "What are you up to these days. You know you had so much promise as a journalist. What a shame you walked away from a great career." I confessed that I was temporarily hairdressing again after having just come out of the forces and Bob must have noticed the fleeting glimpse of regret on my face about my newspaper career.

"Tell you what, how about I make an unofficial approach to Mrs Browning to give you another chance, Terry?" he offered, and I was secretly delighted at the chance to renew my former career. A few days later, I sat in front of Mrs Browning again.

"Firstly, Terry, I have to say I was extremely disappointed when you left us three years ago, not only because you had a promising career but also in the manner you left," she started by giving me a little telling off. "However, we do believe you had great potential and you'll be pleased to know we are prepared to give you another chance," she smiled. It was not just another shot at journalism. It was a reporter role, which meant that I would be starting as a reporter without the benefit of the training the others had undertaken. I was to start on a wage of nine pounds a week. Within months of general reporting, I was accepted as a fully fledged member of the editorial team and even better, was moved into the sports department, which had long been my coveted role. A few months more and I found myself promoted to Sports Editor of the *Dagenham Post*. I could not have been happier that I had turned down a military career.

At the time, my friend George Dudley was making a name for himself as a fullback for Walthamstow Avenue football club and had moved to Dagenham, where I was heavily involved with the Dagenham Football Club, which at that time was playing in the Corinthian League. (They have since recently been promoted into the Football League for the first time in their history!) Because I was involved with the club for work, our social life also become inextricably entwined with the club, with George, Mavis, Jean, and I travelling to away games and involved in club events. George and I had been great mates for years and now we made a tight-knit little foursome that became even tighter when we decided to experience one of Britain's most free-spirited rites of passage together – a trip to the continent, quite a brave venture in the late '50s. A beaten-up VW caravanette was to be our ticket to adventure. By day, we drove through the lush countryside of France, Italy and Switzerland, shopping for fresh vegetables, cheese and meat at local villages (we had a budget of just £50), washing in streams and attending to more personal daily necessities in the forest. By night, the four of us slept side-by-side in the one and only double bed the caravanette contained. Our nights were frequently interrupted by George's sleep-talking, which was often a garbled mix of cockney interspersed with whatever language he was trying to learn that week. Although he tried his hand at French, Italian and German, he added the suffix "mate" to everything, which only confused his intended conversationalists. "Bonjour mate, four croissants mate, merci-beaucoup mate," was his general style and was modified only slightly for Italian. It was my first taste of the great wide world beyond England, and I relished it. When we reached Cannes, we wildly threw off our clothes and ran to the sea, diving and splashing in the warm waters, which are so foreign to the English.

When we reached the Alps we were overawed by their majesty and quite daunted by the task of parking the van in the hilly terrain. One night, after we had traversed a particularly steep piece of country, I was woken from my slumber by George yelling, "Shit Terry, we're rolling. We're bloody rolling down the hill." He sat bolt upright and, in a flash, so did I. I threw myself over the startled bodies of the girls to reach the front seat and the offending handbrake before I realised that George was fast asleep and we were not rolling at all. Thankfully, my burst of action had not caused us to actually start rolling downhill!

The girls were thrilled by the romance and allure of Italy and the foreign sophistication it promised – sometimes it was a sophistication that was a bit much for George and me (and one that led to my second altercation with a "vinegar" bottle). After weeks of eating on the run in the van, we decided to splurge on a slap-up Italian meal. Anyone who has ever been to Italy will know that the Italians forgo butter in favour of dipping their lovely ciabatta or panini bread in olive oil and vinegar. This gives the bread a delicious nutty flavour and, "when in Rome" as they say…so I was keen on devouring this treat. Unfortunately, I had never encountered wine served in a decanter before.

"Spaghetti marina mate and veal saltimbocco per favore mate, and vino bianco mate," George ordered.

"Lasagne and frutii de mare, per favore," I added the mains order for Jean and myself. As is customary, the bread was brought to the table and we set about making our repast. When the waiter bought the wine to our table, I was certain the unusual shaped bottle contained vinegar and was horrified when George began filling our wine glasses with its contents. With the puzzled waiter looking on, I sheepishly emptied each glass back into the bottle only for the waiter to pick up the bottle and refill our wine glasses – it was wine after all. Thankfully, years of travelling the world and dining with sophisticated and influential people has given me a better sense of etiquette and I think my mistakes in the finer points of vinegar use are all behind me.

WEDDED BLISS

In 1959, two little words were to change my life forever and definitely for the better.

"Do you Terence Charles Hopley take Jean Rosina Flavin to be your lawful wedded wife?" the priest looked at me expectantly as I confidently answered with those two poignant words: "I do." I can't say that I knew I would marry Jean from the moment I met her, but I can say that I'm awfully glad that I did. She is my best friend, despite our very different personalities, and we have stayed together through thick and thin, which is almost entirely due to her effort and patience. In those days, getting married was just something you did once you had been together for a year or more, and we entered into marriage very lightly. We had been together for three years, but Jean was just eighteen and I was a fresh-faced kid of twenty-one when we tied the knot at the Church of St Thomas More in Barking. What did we know about life or what the future might hold? I guess that is true of any marriage, but we are among the lucky ones, our future held us together. Our wedding was lovely and special, as all weddings are, but it was far from lavish. Jean's mum made the bridal gown and the bridesmaids' dresses. I wore a suit, as did my best man, my brother Sam. On account of the fact that we received a dividend on the money we spent on food and drink, we held our reception at the Co-op Hall in Dagenham. However, whatever our budget was it clearly wasn't enough and I had to have a whip-round among my mates halfway through the evening so we could continue to get merry late into the night.

Our honeymoon was spent in a caravan (although this time, it warranted more privacy than we had enjoyed in the caravanette with George and Mavis – only a little more though!). We paid about six quid for a week at Dovercourt

Bay, but when we arrived the caravan was so rickety that the bed fell apart in the middle of the night (well, we were on honeymoon). Even worse, when we woke up the next morning and stepped out into the crisp morning air, I was greeted by a familiar face.

"Hello, Tel" my mother used my nickname affectionately. She had decided a week in Dovercourt might suit her and Sheila as well!

Six months before we married we'd bought our first house – a modest, two-storey semi-detached house in Collier Row, Romford – and privacy was scarce even there because we had to rent out upstairs to pay the mortgage. As there was no bathroom or toilet downstairs, Jean and I braved the English winter chill and crept out to the outside toilet (or "dunny" as I should say now that I live part of the year in Australia) to make our privations. Washing was a quick dip in the kitchen sink. To raise the deposit I had scraped together whatever funds I could manage and borrowed the rest from my brother and elder sister. Sam forked out £100 and Jessie £200, but there was no point asking Sheila – she was skint, as always. It seems like a pittance now, but the house cost £2400, which still left a hefty mortgage in those days. When we bought it, the house was in a state, so before anyone could move in we had to renovate it. It took us some months, starting with the top storey and then moving downstairs.

"Nice work, Admiral," Roy Dudley raised his right hand to his forehead in a salute when he saw Jean's choice of attire. She was decked top to toe in a paint-splattered admiral's uniform, with her curls springing out of the jaunty cap. "Here you go," she frisbeed him a top hat and threw a long, tailed jacket at him, "Get into that lot."

The man who sold us the house made his living from buying uncollected clothes from drycleaners and selling them on. He'd left us huge piles of garb including everything from evening gowns to military uniforms. They came in handy when we were undertaking messy renovating jobs, although if anyone had seen us they must have thought we were bonkers. Roy was our chief renovator and interior designer, so was a frequent guest. I was pleased that the former owner had also left behind a piano and Roy was thrilled too because he was keen to learn. I promised him that I would teach him Beethoven's *Fur Elise* before Jean and I got married. At 10 pm each night, we crawled out of our bespattered uniforms and adjourned to the piano. Of course, Jean was still living at her parents in Dagenham and it was about a half hour each way from Romford to Dagenham, so each evening I ferried them both back to their respective abodes on my second-hand NSU scooter. Only one could fit as a pillion passenger, so I used to ferry Jean home first, leaving Roy to stay on and practise the first two bars of Beethoven's classics for an hour until I returned. We were renovating for six months, but he never got past the first two bars, and he still hasn't!

Jean and I were very proud of that little house in Romford, but I was nervous that I had bitten off more than I could chew. The upstairs tenants paid the mortgage but it needed a lot of work to bring it up to scratch and I had neither the money nor the skill to undertake it. Jessie's husband Mick was a born renovator and when he offered to buy it and give us a healthy profit I didn't hesitate. We moved back in with Jean's mum and dad until we could find a newly-built home that didn't require too much maintenance. A few months later we took out a 25-year mortgage of £3000 and moved to County Park Estate, Hornchurch. The chalet-style house had a shared drive with our new neighbours, Mike and Nina Prior – a lovely, fun couple who became life-long friends. The neat little houses of County Park Estate were popular with newlyweds and soon Geoff and Judith Hurst moved in as well. We also forged firm friendships with West Ham United favourites, such as Martin and Kathy Peters, John and Janice Sissons, Ronnie and Dawn Boyce, and Brian and Janice Dear. Many of these friendships have stood the test of time. With friends such as Geoff Hurst (who was playing right half for West Ham, albeit intermittently) and Martin Peters (who often filled Geoff's No. 4 shirt when Geoff was dropped), it was little surprise that I lived and breathed the Hammers in the early 1960s, and it definitely influenced my career in journalism.

THE HAMMERS

Football, which the Aussies and Americans know as soccer, is England's national game. Forget cricket or rugby, "poms" support one football team for life and with a passion that is unmatched by the fans of any other sport. I was no exception. I was the sports editor of the *Dagenham Post* after all, and I was helped in my reporting by my footballer mates. My friend and neighbour Mike Prior also worked as a rep for British Eagle Airways – often the airline of choice for England and West Ham football teams – so they all passed me insider information on the Hammers. At the time, the newspaper group that owned the *Dagenham Post* was rapidly expanding and becoming involved with a new radio station, Capital Radio. Mrs Browning, the company chairperson, had passed away and the group was taken over by her son Alec and daughter Valerie, who had brought in a new right-hand man, Bill Beets. Bill was ambitious and forward thinking – the sort of man I admired – and was keen to listen to my suggestions. At the time, every local paper had a separate sports department, which often meant that several reporters within the group were sent to cover the same event and write it up for separate papers. This seemed like overkill to me, so I conceived the idea of having one sports department across the whole group and then distributing the stories accordingly. Bill liked my idea, and who was made group sports editor? Yours truly, of course. Not only did I get the chance to cover First Division Football games (this was before the birth of the Premier Division), I also got a hefty pay rise and even got to write up England games. I was thrilled and the goings on of the Hammers and the England team became my daily fix. My obsession with the team in the early sixties also helped take my mind off the personal pain Jean and I endured as we struggled to start a family.

A series of unfortunate events brought a sharp sense of loss to our marriage, and it was only years later, with the birth of our daughter Michelle in 1963, that Jean and I were able to begin to heal some of the pain we felt in those early years. Jean became pregnant for the first time soon after we married, but she was only a few months into the pregnancy when an accident in my Renault Dauphine ended in tragedy. It seemed no more than a slight bump, when another vehicle hit the back of our car while we were stopped at traffic lights, but the next day Jean was rushed to hospital and two days later she had a miscarriage. Her second pregnancy began normally, but when she was about four months pregnant, she was again admitted to hospital. This time she was kept in for nine weeks before we were given the awful news that the baby had died. Cruelly, Jean had to endure an induced miscarriage. We were both emotionally drained for months afterwards. During those difficult times, football was a panacea as well as a passion.

When I started covering the team in 1962, the Hammers were far from the most inspiring team. Few thought their new manager, Ron Greenwood, would be ruthless enough to propel them forward. But things quickly changed. First, Greenwood bought Johnny "Budgie" Byrne from Crystal Palace and then had a remarkable stroke of luck when Geoff Hurst (who had been in and out of the team with little idea of what the future there held for him) turned down a move to Crystal Palace in part exchange. Despite Geoff's reluctance to leave the club, the team was still not playing at its best, and when Geoff was called into Greenwood's office following one dismal performance in the reserves, he feared the worst. Thankfully, he was in for a pleasant surprise and was told he was being recalled to the first team as a centre forward. Playing in the number ten shirt (to partner Byrne) as a striker transformed Geoff – and the fortunes of West Ham. Whether Ron Greenwood really saw Geoff's potential as a striker or it was just a desperate experiment born out of a series of poor results remains unknown, but whatever the cause, it paid huge dividends. The fact that the club had tried to sell Geoff off just a short time before led me to believe that Greenwood just got lucky with his experiment. Who knows the truth? Personally, I always found Ron Greenwood a difficult man to get to know. Tactically, he probably knew more about the game than any coach in the world, but in my opinion his man-management skills left a lot to be desired. I also know that key members of the team shared my view. With better management, the world cup firm of Bobby Moore, Martin Peters and Geoff Hurst could have formed the dynamic backbone of the team for a lot longer. Whatever Greenwood's shortcomings, West Ham won the FA Cup in 1964, with Geoff banging in goals by the score. The fans (including me) were ecstatic. The following year, the Hammers became the European champions, beating Munich 1860 in a memorable final of the European Cup Winners Cup at Wembley Stadium. Then, of course, in 1966 Geoff took the field for England and propelled himself to glory with a perfect hat-trick, scoring his first goal with his head, the second with his right foot and the third with his left. It was an impressive performance that still sees my old mate signing autographs and in demand for personal appearances around the world – even though he has reached his three score years and ten. I was proud of Geoff's success and added a new dimension to our sports section in his honour. Geoff and I wrote the "Geoff Hurst Column" in his front room every Sunday afternoon. Of course, the glory belonged to Geoff, but I like to think that some of the reflected glory belonged to me. The column was a popular, and sometimes controversial, feature in the newspaper group's sports pages and sales of our newspapers were climbing steadily. Then, the unthinkable happened for the Hammers. Greenwood sold Martin Peters to Tottenham, Bobby Moore to Fulham and, later, Geoff Hurst to Stoke. He also missed the opportunity to sign Gordon Banks when he was clearly the best goalkeeper in the world. The Hammers reign stalled, but a tragic event was to ensure that my career was propelled firmly forward with all the precision of one of Geoff's famed penalty kicks.

Out of the blue, Hugh Howton, the man who had given me my first break in journalism, died of a heart attack. It was a great loss for the group and there was much speculation and politicking about who would, or could, replace him as the new group editor in chief. It never really crossed my mind that I might be that person, even when I received a surprising call to attend a board meeting.

The meeting began with Bill Beets casually questioning me on my views on the quality of the various newspapers within the group and how I saw the future of the company.

"Now tell me, quite candidly, who you feel should be appointed our new group editor in chief."

Even then I didn't consider myself a candidate as I glibly discussed the strengths and weaknesses of our various editors before telling him, "If it were my decision, I would not promote from within. I would advertise the position nationally."

"We're not going to advertise the position," Bill paused and looked at me directly. "We have already made up our minds. The job's yours if you want it."

I was staggered by Bill's response. I was to be the group editor-in-chief of Greater London and Essex Newspapers. Me! I was astounded, but equally ambitious to make a go of this fantastic opportunity. My promotion also meant that someone had to replace me as group sports editor. Luckily, it was an easy choice. My number two, Len Whaley, filled the spot with distinction. Len's team was Millwall, but his real love was boxing and he became – and still is – one of the most knowledgeable and respected boxing columnists in the business. He still writes a weekly boxing column. When he emailed me to congratulate me on the milestone of turning 70, he quoted boxing promoter Micky Duff, saying, "You don't realise how young 60 is until you reach 70". I couldn't agree more. However, at the time I was just a young upstart and my new role put me in charge of editors who had been far senior to me in the pecking order for years, and few of them liked it. I had big plans and some of them were not included. The newspaper group was more than 100 years old and, in my opinion, was desperately in need of a contemporary shift. One of my first tasks was to weed out some of editors I felt were not up to it and replace them with my own, more modern "disciples". One of my first appointments (at the time considered controversial) was to make an enterprising young editor named John Clarke my deputy. It did little to make me more popular with the staff, but it did kick off the change the group needed. Although I didn't know it yet, it would also prove one of the best decisions I ever made, because John was not only extremely competent, he was later to become my successor, leaving me free to pursue a career that would be the most fulfilling I had ever undertaken.

In the printing works, I was seen as a young pup and it was a real challenge to get on the right side of seasoned compositors who were old enough to be my father. It didn't help that I'd taken the nail off my big toe while mowing the lawn, so had to start the first week of my new job wearing sandals with a hole cut out for my red and swollen toe.

"He doesn't just think he's Jesus Christ, he's even wearing his sandals now," one disgruntled compositor groaned as I walked into the printing works on my first day.

LIFE IN THE FAST LANE

Not even 30 years old and in charge of the editorial department of a newspaper group that was to expand to eighteen titles and a share of Capital Radio – you might think I would have been satisfied, but there was still something lacking in my life and ambition burned away inside my head. It was to be years before I would figure out that what was missing was some serious wealth, but at least I was already on a fast-track to success. My new role was primarily administrative, but for my own professional (and financial) satisfaction I retained a few journalistic roles: reporting on West Ham and England matches and appointing myself motoring correspondent. As Rodney Bennett-England had discovered years earlier, the position of motoring correspondent came with the perk of always driving a top-of-the-range model such as a Porsche, Ferrari or Jaguar courtesy of the manufacturer. The new role also came with a secretary, a wonderful woman named Margaret Ryan, who, along with her husband Jim, remains a close friend. In those days, car manufacturers all kept a fleet of "press" vehicles that they loaned out for road tests, and part of Margaret's job was to schedule my diary to ensure I was never without a flash set of wheels. Of course, this also meant that she often had to take a train to the London showrooms of some of the posh car manufacturers and drive back, often through heavy traffic, in some seriously expensive cars. Poor Margaret never complained, but she often suffered at the wheel of some of my tasty pieces of machinery, as she was not the most confident of drivers, a fact that she admits. The only time I ever heard her come close to complaining was when I sent her to pick up one of those futuristic-looking D21 Citroens.

"What kept you Margaret? I was getting worried," I enquired when my red-faced, heavily perspiring secretary arrived back in the office very late at night after being sent on her mission.

"I wound up in a cul-de-sac, and do you think for the life of me I could find the bloomin' reverse in that ridiculous thing!" she sighed. "I spent ages trying to find reverse and then had to knock on the door of a nearby house to find out if they knew where the reverse on a D21 Citroen was. Of course, no one did, so we had to push the car backwards until we'd made a three-point turn."

The thought of slim, elegant Margaret and her good Samaritans pushing around a luxury car in the dark made me break into a chuckle, but it was quickly stifled by the look on Margaret's usually smiling face.

Because the Ford Motor Company was based in Dagenham and the *Dagenham Post* was one of our best-selling titles, we enjoyed a good relationship with Ford in particular. "Terry Hopley? Graham Simons calling. I'm a public relations officer for the Ford Motor Company and I wondered whether you might be able to help me out. We have a new Granada being introduced and we would like to use Geoff Hurst for the photoshoot. I know that he is a friend of yours and wondered if there might be any chance he would attend a photoshoot at Brands Hatch on Sunday morning?"

"Leave it to me. No problem," I answered, my brain ticking over with how I might use this opportunity to Geoff's advantage and, of course, my own.

"What do you think we would have to come up with to use his image on the advertising?" Graham enquired.

"How about a new top of the range Granada, with all the extras of course."

"It's a deal," he sounded relieved, probably thinking Geoff Hurst could command much more than that.

"Great! Do you think you could manage one for Geoff as well," I added, without missing a beat. And so it was that Geoff and I both got new Granadas. It was, however, a win-win situation, because Ford's new prestige car also exceeded all expectations. The Ford press office also came through with the goods when Jean and I planned our second trip to the French Riviera, travelling along with Roy Dudley and his wife Mary. We were holidaying for three weeks, which was a long time for any road test, so I was fermenting ideas on how I could persuade Ford to lend me a new car for that timespan. While I was formulating a plan, I received a call from another friend who worked at Ford's PR office, Chris Madeley.

"Terry, not to be presumptuous, but I need to ask a favour of you…" he started, which set my mind at ease, knowing the big favour I wanted to ask him in return.

"My son Richard is about to leave school and is desperate to be a journalist and I wondered whether you might be able to set him up with some work experience with a local paper?"

I could see this situation gradually improving to my advantage. Chris and his lovely Canadian wife lived near Brentwood, where my group ran the *Brentwood Argus*, and a simple phone call to the editor Brian Davies was all it took to set Richard Madeley on his path to what would be an illustrious career. In return, I got to borrow a new Granada Executive for three weeks and Richard Madeley got the interview that paved the way for his brilliant future, which would later lead to television. At any rate, it was not long before I recognised that Richard Madeley had the potential to really shine in journalism, so before his twentieth birthday I promoted him to assistant editor of the *East London Advertiser* – one of the biggest papers in the group. I was not to be disappointed, he was an excellent journalist, as time has revealed. He doesn't even know how he got that initial interview, but he was kind enough to give me a mention in the joint autobiography he published with his wife Judy Finnigan.

At the time, I was quite a big fish in a not-too-small pond and I quickly became entrenched in the local community. I was president of the local Rotary Club, president of a national children's charity, a prominent member of the Guild of Newspaper Editors and a regular speaker at the Newspaper Society, an organisation for newspaper proprietors. The highlight of my time with Rotary (I am still an honorary member of the Rotary Club of Dagenham) was organising a youth festival in the borough. More than 5000 youngsters took part and I was glad to give something back to the community I had lived in as a boy. The money raised was used to set up a fund for needy children that, as far as I know, is still running to this day. However, the organisation that proved by far the biggest surprise was the British Majorettes Association, of which I had inadvertently become president. As the editor-in-chief I was constantly being asked to be part of some or other organisation, and in the case of the majorettes I had little idea what they actually did or stood for, but said yes anyway. Turns out my association with the group nearly put me in prison, and in the most unlikely manner!

Because I was the president, Jean and I had received a rather flash-looking invitation to a big parade being held in honour of the Queen's silver jubilee in 1977. About a week beforehand, one of my uncles, who has since passed away, had fortuitously called to say he had some beautiful handmade mohair gents suits and had put one aside for me, as he knew it would fit. A day or so later, I dropped into his East London home and, sure enough, the suit fitted like a glove and I bought it for twenty quid, which was clearly about a tenth of what it was worth. It was a very distinctive suit because it had patch pockets, which were very unusual in those days. Although I had no idea of the importance of the majorette's parade, because the invitation looked quite formal I wore my new suit for the occasion. When Jean and I arrived at St James' Park, we were astonished at the size of the crowd. Tens of thousands of people had turned up to watch the show. Sure that our fancy invite had not intended that we simply stand amid the throngs, I politely pushed my way through the crowd to the nearest bobby and showed him the invitation.

"Yes, yes," he confirmed. "Hang on a second while I check where you're supposed to be." He immediately got on the radio to figure out where we were to sit. Inside the entrance to Buckingham Palace were rows of seats for officials and dignitaries, with two large gilt thrones upholstered in red velvet in the middle for the Duke and Duchess of Gloucester, who were the guests of honour. It didn't take long for the policeman to be informed that was where Jean and I were supposed to be and we hurriedly stuffed the packed sandwiches we had naively brought with us in the bin as we were escorted to an official police car. Within a matter of minutes, we were being whisked to the palace where an equerry ran up (it turns out they had been waiting for us) and said, "Mr Hopley, pleased to meet you. Today you will be sitting next to the Duke. So when the royal car arrives we would like you to go down and greet His Royal Highness and then when he goes to sit, you are to sit on his left there. Your wife…Jean is it?" the equerry extended his hand to my, by now flabbergasted, wife, "You will be sitting next to the Lord Mayor of London, just down the other end there."

I felt hopelessly inadequate all of a sudden and a cold sweat broke out over the back of my neck (under the mohair suit), as I hoped beyond hope that the duke didn't have too many questions to ask about the British majorettes! My shy little Jean had been whisked away out of sight to take her place next to the lord mayor, but soon arrived back on the arm of an equerry with her face red, looking, for all the world, scared stiff.

"Sir," the equerry informed me, "We've just been informed that the Duchess of Gloucester is unwell and will not be attending today. So we would ask that your wife does us the favour of sitting next to the Duke."

All of a sudden, before we knew it, here were Jean and I – a humble pair who had grown up in council houses in Dagenham – sitting each side of the Duke of Gloucester! Even better, because Jean was sitting in a red-velvet chair, thousands of people in the crowd must have thought that my wife was the duchess. My fears about the duke quizzing me in detail about the activities of the British majorettes were also unfounded. He turned out to be a comical and friendly fellow who spent most of his time making rather appreciative comments about some of the majorettes, in between regaling us with stories about life as a royal.

"One thing you never do when you're a royal is walk past a men's toilet. You always go in because you never know when you'll see another one," he laughed, perhaps seeing the strained look on my face. Once the parade had finished and everyone had departed the royal dais, with our nerves shattered, Jean and I turned to each other and burst into relieved laughter. We had made it through one of the most bizarre and surprising days of our lives – little knowing that it was yet to get even more bizarre. When we got home and turned on the television to relive our moment of royal ascension, I saw just how close I could have come to ending up in the nick instead of on the royal dais. The parade was featured in the nine o'clock news and showed us in all our glory, including a good shot of me stepping forward to greet the duke in my handmade French mohair suit. Jean and I were both pretty chuffed by that, until we saw the show immediately following the news. It was a show called Police Five, in which a bloke named Shaw Taylor implored the public to help solve various crimes.

"Finally tonight…last week a van carrying some very expensive French suits was stolen from the car park of a café. The hand-stitched mohair gent's suits are very distinctive, with patch pockets. Anyone offered one should contact their local police station immediately," Shaw Taylor urged, as the screen switched to a close-up of the suit – the same style that I'd just been recorded wearing on the nine o'clock news! Thankfully, Shaw Taylor could not have been watching the news or it might have turned out very differently. The close call didn't stop me wearing the suit for years afterwards – after all, it meant something very special to me. That was not to be my only involvement with royalty. I was soon asked to be a member of a Royal Charities Committee and was invited to attend the birthday party of Prince Charles. He too turned out to be an intelligent, down-to-earth gentlemen and a kind-hearted one as well. While I was chatting with him, an equerry approached and told him that there was a 90-year-old lady downstairs who shared his birthday. Prince Charles suggested that they should bring her up, but when informed that she was too frail to climb the stairs he excused himself and bounded down several flights of stairs to wish her many happy returns. Now that's good grace.

IN LOVE AGAIN

Back in September 1963, I fell in love again. I would say it took me completely by surprise, but, in fact, my love affair with this beautiful girl was at least nine months in the making. Michelle Hopley came into this world on 13 September 1963 and took my breath away. Jean and I could not have been more proud. Proud and happy I may have been, but I have to confess that, for at least the first few months, I was also scared stiff. I didn't want anything to jeopardise the health of this bouncing little bundle of joy, so I even wore a surgical mask around her for the first six months of her life! Like all new parents, we erred on the side of obsession and I don't think I have ever had a stronger relationship with a chemist than I had when my little girl was in her infancy. We doted on her and she rewarded us with smiles, giggles and the usual baby capers. She looked like Jean, with the same impish inquisitive squint, which gave her an air of always having something on her mind, and she usually did. Although she had Jean's gorgeous smile, she was much more extrovert than her shy mother and I don't think she's ever been quiet since the time she learned to talk. I never tire of listening to her, especially now that she remains in England and I don't quite see enough of her.

If you've not noticed already, I'm immensely satisfied with my life and my achievements. I've had significant business success, a number of rewarding careers and made enough money to provide me with the comfort to be able to sit back and reflect today. However, my proudest, most-rewarding achievements are my children. Michelle's brother made his entry into the world just two years later in August 1965. He was such a blond bomber of a boy, despite being two months premature, that I just had to name him Terry Junior. To his credit, Terry has always had his own inimitable way of thinking. He takes things very literally and deeply. He also looks like me and has carried on the name with distinction, enjoying a number of years as something of a playboy in his teens before settling down to family life. He is now a canny businessman. My children, and now the grandchildren (and great granddaughters), are truly my legacy more than any other.

My family life was not the only thing exciting me in 1963, I was also fast becoming the best in the business when it came to covering football. Of course, I had a distinct advantage that few other sports journalists enjoyed – close friendships with the star players. I relished my role and my relationship with Geoff Hurst, Bobby Moore, Martin Peters, Harry Redknapp and Johnny Sissons and counted them as close mates. I was even invited to be the godfather of Johnny Sisson's children, and I still catch up with him occasionally in South Africa. Even more than that, there was a bond of trust between players and travelling journalists that was never broken. They knew they could trust me as a reporter and a friend and that I would not carve them up. Whether journalists were more ethical then than now I don't know, but I do know that we worked under a code of conduct and that I often knew more about what was going on off the field than West Ham manager Ron Greenwood did! Just about everything the boys got up to was on my radar, but I didn't spill the beans. (And don't worry boys, I still won't!) That kind of strong relationship between players and journalists is rare today, when reporters are always looking for dirt and players speak only through their agents. In my opinion, travelling with the team, reporting on games and writing football columns really wasn't work – it was sheer fun. I really enjoyed writing up West Ham games, but whether anybody ever read my articles was another thing.

HAMMERS CHANGE
The Hammers made three changes for the big game at Old Trafford last night but eventually decided to play in claret and blue shirts and white shorts.

The boys and I had taken to playing around with my articles to see whether anyone noticed. There was not a titter from our loyal readers about that one.

The second half of the match was so exciting that neither spectator left before the end.

Still nothing!

Police caught several youngsters climbing over the fence at Upton Park on Saturday. They were forced to climb back into the ground and watch the second half.

No one even noticed. Makes you wonder whether we had any readers at all! The pranks were not just on paper of course. Travelling with the team opened itself up to a range of humorous incidents. In those days, before the expediency of the internet or computers, whenever we travelled we had to ring in our stories. This was made extremely difficult on one trip that the late Peter Lorenzo and I made to Moscow to follow an England game. Between 1 and 2 pm it was impossible to get through to London and we joked that it was because the KGB men were on their lunch break at that time, so couldn't listen in. It was generally reckoned that the Russians had bugged the telephones in our hotel rooms.

"I have 300 words for you on the team tomorrow," Peter rang through to his office with a preview piece for the game.

"Never mind the team. Did you get the microfilm?" the playful copytaker quipped.

"Don't be stupid!" Peter's face went a pasty shade. "Someone could be listening!"

"X, you are instructed to meet Y at…"

Peter slammed down the phone and we sat there waiting for the KGB to storm in and haul us away for interrogation. Thankfully, they never did, so perhaps they weren't listening after all.

KGB agents aside, travelling with the England team gave me a break from the day-to-day demands of running newspapers. One of the most exciting trips was accompanying the players to the 1970 FIFA World Cup in Mexico. As the world cup approached, I was invited to a reception hosted by Shaw International Sports and Travel. The company planned to attract 3000 English supporters to fly to Mexico to see their team defend the Jules Rimet Trophy. It gave me another opportunity to use my marketing acumen to my advantage.

"We have Harold Shepherdson, the England trainer, as our guest of honour at our five promotional evenings," they boasted when I rang to RSVP.

"Who wants to see the England trainer?" came my quick reply. No disrespect to Harold, but this was no way to promote their ambitious programme of attracting that many supporters, flying them around the world and convincing them they had the insider edge.

"Best we could do," the promoter answered, with a disappointed, slightly edgy tone.

"Tell you what…" I said, knowing that this was another of those rare opportunities to provide solutions to their problem while scoring myself a good deal, "…how would you like me to tip up with Bobby Moore, Geoff Hurst, Martin Peters and Peter Bonnetti? And, I am prepared to take care of all five of your future promotions in return for an all-expenses paid trip for five people to Mexico – one ticket for each evening."

To the promoter's credit, he agreed and every one of the five promotional evenings was a rip-roaring success. The first one of these was held at a country club and holiday resort owned by a man who would later become my guiding light, businessman Jack King. He taught me more about business than anyone I had ever met and made me realise what was missing in my life – serious wealth. There was no mistaking that Jack King would make a valuable friend and mentor, and I made sure that he was booked into the same hotel I shared with the England team players in Mexico.

Unlike the current crop of WAGs (wives and girlfriends of the team), who practically ran the show in Germany in 2006, the then English manager, Sir Alf Ramsey, was not keen on the idea of players' wives travelling to Mexico. For this reason, the five tickets I had procured were, of course, not for the players but for Tina Moore, Judith Hurst, Kathy Peters, Frances Bonetti, and me. I was truly one of the inner circle as I drove the girls to the airport, kitted out in a new pigskin trench coat. These trench coats were something of a status symbol with the privileged football fraternity in those days and mine was measured up for me personally by Bobby Moore, who had become involved with the company that made them. Due to Alf Ramsey's disapproval, the girls had to stay out of town, but once we touched down I made my way to the Guadalajara Hilton, where the team had already gathered.

I was sharing a room with Terry McNeil, a reporter for *News of the World*, and we headed straight to the restaurant for lunch. Thinking I was playing it safe, I chose beef stroganoff for my first Mexican meal. It was a big mistake. Just as I was mopping a piece of bread over the remains of my delicious meal the team arrived in the dining room direct from a training session.

"Don't touch the beef stroganoff. Everyone who has eaten it has died a thousand deaths," Geoff yelped when he spotted me. It was too late. I was sick for the next two days and the only saving grace was that at least the toilet and bathroom sink were in close enough proximity that I could discharge into both simultaneously. It made for an extremely uncomfortable 48 hours and even the best efforts of the England team doctor could not remedy my bout of food poisoning.

Despite that setback, the experience of being in a soccer-crazy country like Mexico for a World Cup Tournament was unforgettable. Even in the press box the buzz was electric. I didn't see him personally but they told me that Prince Philip, Duke of Edinburgh, even came to see how the team's preparation was going as they desperately tried to acclimatise to the scarcity of oxygen at 5000 feet. This is how the story went. The players lounge was on the twelfth floor of the Hilton and, following a particularly gruelling training session, they were all slumped, exhausted, in their armchairs when the royal party arrived.

"Please stand up to meet His Royal Highness," the young equerry, who was preparing the way for the duke, politely requested. They all did so immediately with the exception of that great character and former Aston Villa centre forward Jeff Astle, who remained reclined.

"You'll have to excuse me if I don't stand up," Jeff explained. "We're having a lot of trouble with this altitude. I'm absolutely shattered."

By this time, the duke had arrived and to counter any perceived insult the equerry countered with, "You surprise me, my man. His Royal Highness only arrived on Sunday and played a tough game of polo yesterday with absolutely no ill-effects."

"Ask his fucking horse how he felt!" came Astle's quick, much-lauded reply.

Despite the enthusiasm of the team, particularly players like Alan Ball, whose reaction when told for the first time he would be playing for the England team was, "It'll be ten years before anyone gets that England shirt off my back," it was a disappointing tournament for England. Mind you, so much has been written about England's 3–2 defeat by West Germany (not least by Geoff Hurst, who has penned no less than four bestsellers) that I will refrain from mentioning the matches themselves in favour of mentioning some of the more amusing reports to come from the tournament. During one game featuring Mexico, Brian Glanville, a somewhat-literary sports writer for the *Sunday Times*, delivered a remark that has become a classic for after-dinner speakers in Britain. Glanville's phraseology often gave the impression that he was writing about the Bolshoi Ballet, rather than covering a football match, and he was also purported to be something of a linguist. This particular match was to challenge his command of Spanish. With about five minutes to go, Mexico were desperately clinging to a 1–0 advantage. "Desperate" was the word because their goal was under siege and their manager was on the touchline, screaming, jumping up and down, ranting and literally tearing his hair out.

"What's he saying, Brian?" asked one of the other journalists.

In his most up-market accent, Brian solemnly replied, "He is telling them to keep calm."

I guess I shouldn't be too hard on other sports journalists who covered the 1970 World Cup, because, from a reporting point of view, I always felt I was one step ahead of the opposition. Not only did I have a rapport with the players, I also had a unique relationship with Sir Alf Ramsey. Like me, Alf was a Dagenham boy, and, like me, he often found it necessary to pretend to be something he wasn't. Sometimes, as he was addressing the press, he would catch my eye and I had the uncanny feeling he knew exactly what I was thinking. More to the point, I felt I often knew what he was thinking too. There was an unwritten agreement between us that I broke only once, much to my disadvantage and his disapproval.

Alf had a brother who was a right tearaway and the deal was that I made no reference to him at potentially embarrassing moments. I did it just once, to see what would happen, and Alf was extremely annoyed with me. Nevertheless, he occasionally called me aside to give me a snippet of information that would be something of an exclusive, which made my job a lot easier.

My relationship with Jack King, and his wife Joan and son Geoffrey was also cemented further in Mexico City. After England's defeat I travelled on with them, first to Acapulco and then on to California and Las Vegas. It was my first real taste of the millionaire lifestyle, and I savoured it.

"The reason most people never make any money is that they're too busy working," Jack told me. "If you want to make money you won't have time to work. If you're broke it's easy to be entrepreneurial because you've got nothing to lose."

I hung on his every word as he told me wonderful stories of his climb from rags to riches. I did not fancy the idea of being broke to get there, but the idea of serious wealth, well, that was enticing. Jack had decided that he wanted to get into politics and, within a few years he ran, successfully I might add, to become a Tory member of Essex County Council. At this time, I finally had a chance to repay just a small amount of Jack's generosity by writing his election campaign manifesto. I knew that if he were to be successful he would need to grab people's attention in the first three lines, and I like to think he did. Of course, Jack was not to be outdone and he quickly thanked me by presenting me with a lovely little four-berth caravan at his holiday camp in Canvey Island. I also did another deal with Jack by letting him road test all the cars that came my way from the manufacturers. In return, he let me use his brand-new Rolls Royce Silver Shadow on permanent loan until the day I could afford my own. By that time, the idea of generating serious wealth was high on my list of priorities. I had begun dabbling with business in a number of ways and it would not be long before a silver shadow was on my horizon.

SELLING SPACE

After the thrill of Mexico and Las Vegas, back in the office I had more-run-of-the-mill matters to attend to. Many people think being a journalist or editor is glamorous or exciting, and in some respects it is, but, like any job, there are mundane elements to being group editor-in-chief that few people think of; one of these is filling advertising space. I was left in no illusion by the board that our primary role was to make a profit, and that meant selling ads. Advertising is really the main focus of newspaper and magazine publishing and has tremendous monetary value for a newspaper group. What is not filled with advertising is left over for editorial, which is produced with the sole aim of building the newspaper's circulation. Cancellation of advertising at the last minute, or news stories that fall down unexpectedly result in empty space, which has to be filled. Additionally, articles don't always fit together nicely on the page, leaving other awkward, blank spaces that are of little value to most advertisers, who want enough room and good positioning to sell their product. These spaces still need to be filled with something and provided me with an opportunity. I owe much of my success to fillers.

For a number of years I had been dabbling in business, partly to diversify and partly to fill the gap in my own life that was not already filled with Jean and the kids, football and running the group. Sounds like there wasn't much of a gap there already, doesn't it? And perhaps there wasn't, but I enjoyed being always on the go and had even dabbled with working nights in Fleet Street for a little while until I seized on the idea of using some of my hard-earned cash to fund businesses of my own.

Hairdressing was something of a family business for the Hopleys, and although I had tried it a few times and it certainly wasn't my cup of tea, it still seemed like a sure bet for a business. As long as hair kept growing, it would need cutting, so I went into partnership with my brother Sam and my sister Jessie to buy a ladies hairdressing business in Dagenham. I like to think that one of my greatest abilities as a businessman is killing two birds with one stone, finding solutions that are not only in my best interest but that of my business partner too. It's something I have had much success at over the years. In this way, the spare space that plagued Greater London and Essex Newspapers would become a boon for my first business venture, providing us with free advertising, even if it was squeezed into small slots. What I hadn't counted on was that siblings sometimes make difficult business partners, and family squabbles are far more stressful than quarrels between unconnected business partners. Sam was already running his own hairdressing salon, which had been set up for him before my dad died years ago, so it was tempting for him to see this shop as another link in his chain, rather than a joint business. To make it worse, his propensity for gambling reared its ugly head and within five minutes, it seemed, we were at each other's throats about who was in charge of finances. Jessie would have made a perfect partner, but fiercely loyal as she was, she was busy rearing a family, which at the last count had grown into three children, fourteen grandchildren and six great grandchilren. Within a very short time I pulled out and left them to it, moving on to another venture that was, this time, only slightly removed from a family interest.

Jean's sister Carol was married by that time to Malcolm, who worked for British Gas as a fitter. On one of his jobs he visited a factory where they made reproduction nests of Queen Anne tables. When Malcolm told me he had been offered one for twenty-five quid I could see an opportunity. The same tables were being sold in Harrod's for £110.

"Jean would love one," I told him and asked him to see if he could get me one at the going wholesale price. Jean was suitably impressed and everyone who saw it thought likewise. We had a number of visitors who expressed their admiration and wanted to know where to get one.

"I tell you what," I approached Malcolm, "Why don't you talk to this guy to see whether he can supply us too, and we'll set up a furniture business and sell these for thirty-five quid?"

Malcolm was reluctant to talk to him, but from my perspective it was a "no-brainer" – the furnituremaker got his twenty-five quid, we made ten quid on each sale, and the public did not have to pay the 110 quid they paid at Harrods. How could it possibly go wrong? Even better, I knew the perfect location for our furniture store – right next door to the office of the *Havering Echo*, a paper in our group. It meant I could pop in to check on both of my interests in Havering at once, the *Echo* and the newly titled Emerson Galleries, a lofty name for a furniture store. In retrospect, the furniture itself was of doubtful quality, but it got the kind of advertising that Harrods and House of Fraser could only dream about and no one seemed to care that a remarkable number of filler ads in Greater London and Essex Newspapers were for a relatively humble furniture shop. We sold more than a half a million pounds worth of furniture that year and Malcolm was involved in the furniture, fixtures and fittings business for the rest of his working life. Eventually, I pulled out of it to concentrate on other enterprises because, profitable as it was, life was too short to be messing around with furniture. As time would tell, I had other, bigger, fish to fry.

When the newspaper group told me they wanted to sell the office of the *Havering Echo*, I conceived the idea of putting another business there instead, so I made them an offer they couldn't refuse. I would take on the lease of the office for Tel Travel, a travel company bearing the shortened version of my name, and they could keep a small office for the *Echo* in the back room. They wouldn't have to pay me any rent for the office; instead, the price for their office space would be more free newspaper advertising, garnering me better positioning than just the space fillers. The travel agency took off in impressive style, mainly due to the disproportionate amount of advertising that came its way. Mavis Dudley, wife of my old mate George, took on the task of running it and made a great success of it, even with absolutely no experience. Meanwhile, Greater London and Essex Newspapers was undergoing a period of expansion, acquiring the Express group of newspapers and another group called News of Essex, which took our little empire from the City of London out as far as Southend-on-Sea. By 1975 the company had also bought a new web offset printing press at Rochford and the aim was to launch free weekly newspapers. You might think that would have proved quite a headache for the group editor-in-chief, and it certainly did – such a headache that we required a new transport company to look after the demands of moving copy and newspapers over the ever-increasing area we serviced. So I started one.

In no time at all, Transvan, as my company was known, had every contract going within the Greater London and Essex Newspaper group and, once again, my fellow directors didn't seem to mind. However, I had not anticipated just what a logistical nightmare collecting, distributing and delivering half a million free newspapers door to door, as well as handling all subscription sales and running a messenger service between offices spread over a 100-mile radius could be. Naively, I had at first figured Mavis could manage the business in addition to Tel Travel. Before long I had Jean, her sister Carol, Mavis and George, my mum, all the kids, both of my sisters and just about every friend we had, including neighbours Eileen Morris and Eunice Church, working for Transvan. I can still see my poor old mum and all her friends now, sitting there all red in the face, rolling newspapers in wrappers for dispatch by post all over the globe.

"Morning Eileen, first thing this morning could you drive to our Fleet Street Office and pick up some pictures from a Mr Hammond." My voice must have sounded impossibly chirpy to poor Eileen Morris as she listened to my tape-recorded message each morning, which went something like this: "Then could you take them to the works at Rochford (about 50 miles). When you've done that, will you drive to Bishop's Stortford (another 50 miles) and pick up some bundles of newspapers that have to be taken to Maidstone (a further 50 miles). Then bring the car home and I suggest you take the train to Mayfair, where there will be a bundle of copy that has to be taken back to Southend (another 100 miles)." Poor Eileen thought she was stepping into a comfortable little job when she joined Transvan, but apparently not. She lasted the pace for quite a few months before she told me what I could do with my job! Eunice lasted a little longer and, with her Barbara Windsor-esque big boobs and blonde hair, was always well received at the printing works, which she routinely brought to a standstill. Transvan was not just a headache for my friends and family, I was heavily involved on the weekends as well and had to manage the hundreds of other delivery staff the company employed, not all of whom were honest. We were constantly finding huge bundles of newspapers stuffed into waste bins and hedges, and I doubt there was ever a week that we got them all distributed. Together with Jean, the kids and George and Mavis, I toiled all day to cover just a very small section of our circulation. We ran all day, delivering papers door to door every weekend, but at the end of the day it always seemed that we had hardly made an impression on the thousands of newspapers in the back of the van. We always ended the day with fish and chips, and believe me, there was never any shortage of wrapping paper! It was at about this time that another business opportunity took the legs right out from under me, quite literally.

WELCOME ABOARD

I received an invitation to dinner on a cruise ship moored at Millwall Docks from Peter Robinson and Peter Richardson, who ran the passenger side of Fred.Olsen lines, which controlled three beautiful cruise vessels – the *Black Watch*, the *Black Prince* and the *Blenheim*. I accepted the invitation and attended with my secretary, Margaret. The invitation was really just a junket where the two Peters could hopefully persuade me to provide them with free advertising in the group in exchange for special fares for our readers, not to mention the nice little incentive of 10 per cent of all revenue. As a result, reader offers in Greater London and Essex Newspapers were born.

As soon as I set foot on board the *Black Watch*, I felt a certain affinity for it that was hard to explain. I felt like I belonged there. My gut instinct, as it turned out, was to prove correct. Margaret, however, didn't quite share my enthusiasm for the ship and her gut instinct made her violently ill all through dinner, despite the vessel being tied up at the time! Either that or it was the fine French wine, which had been supplied in liberal quantities. The *Black Watch* was far from the most luxurious cruise ship in the world at the time, but it did have a tremendously loyal winter following. It crossed backwards and forwards from Millwall to Madeira and the Canary Islands, carrying 400 passengers and returning with a load of tomatoes from Tenerife and Las Palmas and onions from Lanzarote. Each identical cruise lasted thirteen nights, with the fourteenth evening being used to unload cargo on the wharf in London. Fred.Olsen cruise lines unloaded tomatoes and loaded passengers on at that same wharf at every cruise for the next few years. We nicknamed it Canary Wharf, after our cruises' most common destination. Today, that wharf is one of the most prestigious waterside locations in the world.

I had decided to use editorial space to promote the cruise, and was helped in my endeavours by an event that, although unfortunate and annoying at the time, was probably another blessing in disguise. When the group had acquired the Express group of newspapers, they had also acquired a particularly militant group of highly unionised journalists who didn't hesitate to make my life as the boss hell. Newspaper profits had been good for many years, so I suppose it was inevitable that the print unions would then go on the warpath. The Society of Graphical & Allied Trades (SOGAT), National Society of Operative Printers, Graphical and Media Personnel (NATSOPA) and the National Union of Journalists (NUJ), all fell under the influence of the lefties. The only upside was that they abhorred each other almost as much as they hated the publishing companies. Suddenly, some of my old mates in the editorial departments of our newspapers became my enemies. Our unionised journalists and photographers began engaging in needless strikes, set up the dreaded and thankfully now illegal "closed shop", in which only union members could be employed, and carried on with a quaint practice known as "working to rule" – whereby employees would refuse to do anything that was not specifically written up in their employment contract. This led to what I considered ridiculous petty disputes in which journalists would refuse to take their copy to the sub's desk because it was not in their contract! Where once I happily sat and laughed with my friends and colleagues, working together on getting out a good story, suddenly the smiles disappeared and I didn't always feel welcome in the offices, particularly those that were once Express owned. The tyres on my car were routinely let down and once my car literally blew up in the street – the result of sugar being poured in the petrol tank. At that point, I decided enough was enough. I had a working class background and was not unfamiliar with that insecure feeling that I was rising above my station, but I thought I could use my down-to-earth nature to get through to my staff that we were all in this together. Surely this was not something that a few beers and a good chat could not mend.

"Gather round please," I urged the team, plonking my carton of beers down on the table and gesturing for the Express group crew to get up close and personal.

"I don't want this to be a boss to employee chat. We've just bought the group so let's all have a heart to heart and get everything off our chests."

To encourage the kind of relaxed atmosphere I was attempting to create,

I had sat down in an office chair and raised one of my legs up on another chair, inviting my staff to help themselves to a beer.

"Get your f*cking leg off my chair," was the immediate response from one of the charming journalists I had inherited. Needless to say, the problem was more serious than I had imagined.

At this point, Bill Beets, my managing director, recognising the potential problems the unions could make for us, came up with a brilliant masterplan concerning one particular union boss.

"Loves a drink he does," Bill nodded sagely, "Why don't we hold our next meeting with him at the Café Royal over lunch? We'll bring out a few bottles of good wine. He won't know what he is agreeing to after a couple of hours."

When the day of the lunch rolled around, Bill gave me a knowing wink as he ordered a bottle of wine and poured himself and the union man a healthy glass.

"Now, about this issue we're having with working to rule…" I continued, too absorbed in righting the wrongs of British print publishing to notice at first that Bill's winks were becoming all the more frequent, as were his glasses of wine. Soon, Bill was grinning from ear to ear and seemed all too inclined to nod happily as Mr NUJ put forward his best arguments. Bill seemed almost disinterested in any talk of union action, preferring to keep piping up with the suggestion that we move on to a club! To my horror it was my managing director who was sliding off his chair, not Mr NUJ at all! I swear Bill would have handed every employee a share of the company had I not stepped in and brought the meeting to a grinding halt. Despite our lack of success in sweet-talking the union officials, we did have one ace up our sleeve. Because SOGAT hated NATSOPA and both of them hated the NUJ we were usually able to publish regardless of whichever one was on strike. Really, with such a divided front, the journalists didn't stand a chance. The other thing, of course, was that we saved the strikers' salaries and found it surprisingly easy to find enough copy to fill the papers without them. This meant even more free filler ads for Tel Travel, Emerson Galleries, Transvan and, what was to be our newest venture, cruises to the Canary Islands.

SEA SICKNESS

Given the quantities of free space in our newspapers thanks to union action, I instructed every working editor in the group to use a piece I had written about a wonderful, but limited, reader cruise offer and ran it along with a large picture of the *Black Watch*. Of course, I did the honourable thing and told the board of directors that I planned to earn some revenue from the spare space and, although I could have kept the 10 per cent commission for myself, I settled for a free cruise for my family and let the paper keep the profits. The first newspaper to run the promotion was the *East London Advertiser*, which was published on a Friday. The article urged those wishing to book to either send in their deposit cheque or drop in to our office on Mile End Road to pay in person. Friday was a fairly slow day and nothing much happened, but I had asked Margaret to come in to the office to take any deposits, as she was the only person (apart from me), who really knew anything about the promotion.

"Terry, I have £40,000 in the drawer of my desk and there are still people queuing in reception!" Margaret rang in a fluster at about 11 am.

"They are all paying in full, and they are all paying cash!"

It was better than I ever could have imagined. Typical of East Enders they didn't mess about. They recognised the special prices we were offering, loved the thought of cruising directly out of Millwall, which was right on their doorstep, and carried their worldly wealth in readies – a new era in cruising was born.

Cruising, in the early 1970s, was a fairly posh business. Only a certain kind of person could afford to cruise, so the passenger list was commonly made up of major-generals, brigadiers, bishops and the aristocracy. Here I was about to fill a cruise ship with cockneys! Of course today many cruise ships are about as upmarket as Butlin's was in those days and are little more than floating holiday camps, but the *Black Watch* was a stylish little ship.

Dear Passenger,

Thank you for booking on our special reader offer Black Watch *cruise from Millwall in November. We are sure you will enjoy a wonderful trip to the Canary Islands, enjoying the delicious food and exciting entertainment we have arranged for you. I would like to remind you that for days at sea gentlemen are required to wear black tie and ladies evening or cocktail wear. We look forward to welcoming you on board.*

Yours sincerely,
Terry Hopley
Group Editor-in-Chief

I thought it prudent to write to every passenger letting them know exactly what it was they were getting themselves into and, to their credit, they all looked a million dollars at the "Welcome Aboard" cocktail party. The cockney crowd rose to the occasion, with the men in their dinner jackets and velvet bow ties and the ladies in full-length evening gowns. I, for one, wish those days were still with us.

Although the cruise was months away, at the end of November, I soon had to ring Peter Richardson to increase the paper's allocation of cabins and was pleased when he readily agreed. Being a bit naïve about the cruise industry back in those days, I was not aware that cruises leading up to Christmas were always the hardest to sell because all of the regular passengers knew about the terrible weather in the Bay of Biscay at that time of year. It's a pity I didn't!

"Ladies and gentleman, welcome aboard the *Black Watch*," the stewards, all dressed in their crisp blue uniforms helped more than 100 of our excited readers aboard the ship at Canary Wharf. Everyone was eager to get underway and enjoy thirteen days of sunshine and nights of great food and entertainment as the ship sailed on to Madeira, Lanzarote, Tenerife and Las Palmas.

"Now if you'll all please come this way, we would like to get a group photo, which you will receive as a souvenir at the end of your stay." I had organised to have one of the newspaper groups' photographers on board so we could run another editorial feature showing readers at home what they had missed. As another personal gesture and a customer service, I had also arranged to fly copies of some of our titles to Madeira, so our passengers would have a copy of the local paper delivered to their cabin once we arrived. In my experience, these small but personal touches can make all the difference between the success and failure of a business venture.

The first evening on board was a great success. As the ship glided down the smooth waters of the River Thames, we dined on a delectable meal that highlighted why Fred.Olsen lines had such an enviable reputation. We then kicked off the evening entertainment with a show that, just for good measure, incorporated a few good old cockney songs. When the show finished, as we made our way back to our cabins, I was somewhat surprised to see stewards placing what appeared to be Chinese take-away boxes at strategic places on the staircases and lounges. I did not really dwell too much on their actions, although I was soon to discover their significance.

Jean and I were given a luxurious suite at the front of the ship and as the majestic vessel passed by Barking Power Station, Canvey Island Refinery and Southend Pier, we contented ourselves with gazing at the view while sipping cocktails in our suite. I was extremely impressed with the cruise so far and knew we were in for something memorable. We were, but not in the way I had thought!

At 4 am, a great lurch of the ship woke me immediately and I sat bolt upright in bed.

Crash! A second lurch catapulted me right out of the bed. I immediately rushed to the porthole. All I could see was a steep wall of blue-green that slanted at a dangerous angle. We were actually climbing. Up and up we went, higher and higher until we reached twelve metres. Suddenly, the sea appeared to drop out from under us, and we fell heavily, until the ship's bow met the sea again with an almighty crash. Every item in the cabin that was not tied down was now rolling around the cabin floor. Immediately, the climb resumed again, followed by the gut-wrenching fall and the loud crash – this time accompanied by a tremendous vibration as the propellers came out of the water. My first night on board quickly saw me overwhelmed with a sensation worse than fear (some might even say worse than death) – seasickness. It was a subject on which I would become a world authority over the next twenty years, but had I known that at the time I might never had set foot on a ship again! Jean and I clung to the bed like grim death as the ship rattled, crashed and shuddered its way through the night. My only hope was that daylight might bring calm with it, but that was not to be the case. As daylight broke, the situation did not improve and I crawled out of bed to peer out of the porthole, only to be perplexed by the sight I saw, which gave the impression the sea was actually above us. I collapsed back on the bed, convinced that was where I would have to remain until we found a harbour somewhere… anywhere. In the morning, however, Jean discovered she had a much stronger constitution than I did. After her expression of relief that we had not sunk during the night, she began to find the entire experience a bit of a laugh. I watched forlornly as she staggered from one side of the cabin to the other and then attempted to shower and dress amid the swaying. Our friends Roy Dudley and his wife Mary were also onboard and probably experiencing as much misery as we were at that point.

"I'll go find Roy and Mary and see how they are," Jean said, seeing my green complexion and knowing that I would not be going anywhere soon. My white knuckles gripped both sides of the bed like a vice and I kept my head pressed firmly into the pillow to quell my urge to vomit. A few minutes later, Jean returned with Roy in tow.

"Mary's also sick," Jean informed me, "and so must be most of the other passengers. There isn't a soul about out there, Terry."

"You've just got to forget about it, mate," encouraged Roy, who also appeared to have a stronger constitution than I did. "Get up and have a shower and we can go and have some breakfast while the dining room's not crowded," he urged.

I opened one eye for a few seconds, just long enough to consider his proposal – it was also just long enough to see Roy's usual ruddy complexion turn a sickly shade of pale. Turns out his constitution was not so strong after all.

"I can't stay here," he suddenly moaned. "I'll see you later," and he legged it back to his cabin. I learned a valuable lesson about ships on that first voyage – never choose one of the big, luxury suites positioned right at the top at the front of a ship. To see why, simply hold a pencil at its centre and rock it up and down vertically. You will notice that the point of the pencil makes a wide arc, but the centre hardly moves. Roy and Mary's cabin was midship, while ours was right at the sharp end. (I know that argument is weakened somewhat by the fact that Mary was sick as well, but she gets seasick when someone spills tea in a saucer). Eventually, with the aid of an injection from the ship's doctor, I managed to haul myself up and stagger down to the public areas. To my horror and disgust, many of the takeaway boxes were still lying around, but they were no longer empty… The public areas were also bedecked with ropes for those brave enough to attempt to move around. I remembered being told by someone years ago that a suitable cure for seasickness was to go out on deck. That was certainly out of the question. All of the doors to outside areas were out of bounds and there were repeated announcements to refrain from moving around unnecessarily and on no account to try to go out onto the decks. I realised that was sensible advice when I looked out of the window and noticed that the formerly inviting deckchairs were firmly lashed together and the entire deck was being assaulted by crashing waves. Somehow, despite my state, I managed to stumble down to the dining room. Only three forlorn diners were in there, although it should have been the middle of breakfast, and none of them looked particularly hungry. Suddenly, I realised that there were at least 100 'reader offer' passengers on this ship who would gladly kill me this instant if they were well enough. And we had another twelve days of this to go!

"Excuse me," I grabbed weakly at a passing officer. "Where are we exactly?"

"Just off the coast near Eastbourne," the clearly harassed sailor answered.

Just off the bloody coast of Eastbourne? I could have driven there myself in two hours from Millwall. I thought we were in the middle of the North Atlantic! Right at that moment, cruising was not for me.

For a further 24 hours the storm raged on and on. Eventually, the ship's doctor even had to stop giving injections because he was so sick himself. But regardless, the ship crashed on, across the Bay of Biscay with not a soul to be seen in the public areas. Cape Finisterre, thankfully, was the turning point. Suddenly, the officers re-emerged, resplendent in pristine white uniforms, and everyone stopped throwing up. The remarkable thing about seasickness is that when it stops you are not only immediately and overwhelmingly better, you also feel so incredibly happy to be alive. As soon as this miraculous transformation occurs, seasickness sufferers begin to recount their woes, further embellishing the stories of their despair at each telling. One of the best I heard was that a waiter, who was rushing through the lounge carrying a plate of carrot and tomato-laden vegetable soup, stumbled as the ship gave an almighty lurch. Losing his balance, he tripped and spilt the soup all over an unfortunate elderly gentleman who had been fast asleep in a nearby armchair. Quick as a flash the waiter shook the old boy.

"Feeling better now, sir?" he asked him.

And they told me that really happened!

MY SEA CHANGE

The nicest thing about visiting Madeira and the Canary Islands in the middle
of the European winter is that you are almost certain at some point to
experience that magical transition from freezing cold and rain to warmth
and bright sunshine. In just a few hours on my 'maiden voyage' I went from
wishing myself dead to happily playing quoits on deck and swimming in
the pool. My favourite destination on that cruise was Madeira, which had
a wonderful floral landscape, extremely friendly locals and an indefinable
Britishness that resulted from its colonial past. I fell in love with it then and
there, little knowing that I would one day reside there. The rest of the journey
passed smoothly and all of our passengers, including Jean and myself, were
impressed with the high standard of the meals and entertainment. We
were soon on our return voyage, laden with 100,000 boxes of tomatoes,
onions, bananas and potatoes that Fred.Olsen lines ferried back to England.
Thankfully, the fruit and vegetables acted as a kind of ballast and made the
ship much more stable. The sea was also kinder so we didn't experience the
dire seasickness of the outgoing voyage. On our return trip I grew tired of
lazing on deck (typically, for me) and sought permission to visit the bridge.
My position, coupled with the fact that I had put 100 passengers on board,
earned me that privilege and I spent hours there as well as in the engine
room, the galley and the office of the cruise director. I even did my best to
make an ally of the Norwegian captain, Erik Lovet, a serious, stern man who
was always immaculate in his white uniform decorated with gold braid at the
shoulder and on the cap. As his job demanded, he frequently took the time to
stop and chat with passengers and was a real hit with the ladies – that looked
a far better job to me than running newspapers! By the time we arrived back

in Millwall on a cold December morning, the majority of my passengers had completely forgotten about that terrible two-day storm and were so happy that they were just about ready to book another cruise already.

"We are going to charter a cruise ship and run a complete cruise ourselves," I proudly informed the board of Greater London and Essex Newspapers on my return to the office. The board had been very pleased with the £10,000 in commission I had handed them after our toe-in-the-water introduction to reader offers, but they seemed less than enthusiastic about this new idea.

'No, we're not!' Bill Beets rapidly replied. 'We're newspaper publishers and that is all we do."

"But…"

"Forget about it." Bill was adamant.

But I couldn't forget about it. There was money to be made. I had made them an offer they couldn't refuse; yet refuse it they had. If they weren't prepared to take advantage of this opportunity then I certainly was.

"Then I'll charter one myself," I told Bill candidly.

Following a long meeting at the Regent Street offices of Fred.Olsen lines, it was agreed I would charter the *Blenheim*, the sister ship to the *Black Watch*, for a complete cruise. The charter price was well into six figures and I had to take out a second mortgage on our new house at Emerson Park, Essex, to pay the necessary 5 per cent deposit up front. On top of that, all expenses for brochure production, marketing and advertising would be mine. It was a make or break gamble. I had not involved Jean too much in my plans, preferring to ensure things were running smoothly before divulging much information about it. If my plans had fallen apart, it would have been disastrous, both for our finances and our marital peace. Unlike me, Jean was very much a home bird. I had bought us a big, detached five-bedroom home, complete with indoor pool, sauna and games room, and Jean was very content there. She was happy to be a housewife while her hardworking husband came home to the kids every night. However, with me, she never knew what she was going to get. (A fact that would become even more apparent over the next few years!) Still, I figured, the amount Fred.Olsen lines were asking was a fair price and meant that the net cost for each passenger was £300, so all I had to do was find 400 passengers willing to hand over £400–1400 for a cruise – a lot of money in those days. If I were successful, I would pocket £100–£1100 per passenger.

Thankfully, fate took a hand in the form of the NUJ. With my good friends the journalists on strike for the umpteenth time, my senior editorial staff had plenty of space to fill with a huge picture of the cruise ship and a centre spread about this wonderful new cruise that had the backing of the newspaper. Sure enough, the bookings came flooding in and before long, I was home and dry and the ship was completely full. Understandably, there was a good deal of nervousness in the boardroom at my sudden enthusiasm for cruise ships, but, despite this, I felt I had an obligation to be on the ship for my first full charter. On the cruise, I took it upon myself to spend hour after hour on the bridge, applying myself to the economics and practicalities of running a ship. I was extremely curious and interested, getting involved in just about everything that happened on board. I also learned another valuable lesson about cruise ships – the personality of a ship is directly related to the personality of its crew. Although the *Blenheim* and the *Black Watch* were nearly identical in design, both had totally different identities. The *Black Watch* was run mainly by Norwegian officers under the command of Captain Eric Lovet. It also had Norwegian senior staff, with a crew of mostly Portuguese nationals from Madeira. The Norwegians were rather a pragmatic bunch who often didn't find public relations duties simple. Eventually, however, Captain Lovet's position passed to Thor Fleten, the former first officer of the *Black Watch*. He was a much more personable captain, who was excellent at his job and really taught me everything he knew about running a cruise liner. His appointment was considered controversial because he had been known to enjoy a drink, but from the moment he attained that fourth gold band on his shoulder, he never touched alcohol again. The Portuguese cabin crew and catering staff, meanwhile, were tremendous. They were very keen to do everything possible to make passengers happy. On the Blenheim, the officers, staff and crew were all British, under the command of a typically wry Yorkshireman named David Smethurst. David was renowned for his humorous, although often slightly alarming, broadcasts from the bridge.

"Ladies and gentlemen, this is the captain. You are probably wondering why the ship has stopped and all the lights have gone out," came one of his more memorable announcements (and no doubt passengers had wondered!). "I would like to assure you that we have everything under control on the bridge. We plan to spend the rest of the day drifting." And we did!

On another occasion onboard the Blenheim, David really had the passengers wondering what sort of cruise they had signed up for.

"Good afternoon ladies and gentleman, this is the captain speaking from the bridge. I would like to take this opportunity of welcoming you all on board and wishing you a pleasant cruise with us. So that we can leave the berth, would you please all help us out by moving to the starboard side of the ship." Far from being standard procedure, there was method in David Smethurst's madness on this occasion. We were leaving from the Tilbury Landing Stage and the falling tide had wedged the ship's side loading doors up against the wooden quay, meaning the ship was literally stuck fast to the quay. David had simply sucked on his pipe for a few minutes, considering the problem, and then came up with his baffling request. He had even sent some young deck officers through the ship to persuade the passengers to move to the starboard side. Amusing as it was, it worked!

In my opinion, the British officers were the best I worked with and they gave me great support in my endeavours to increase our percentage of repeat passengers over the years. However, the British staff in the dining room and lounges were not so great. They, too, were heavily unionised and their obsession with who did and did not tip often made my life uncomfortable. Staff aside, what truly made the ships of the Fred.Olsen line memorable was the quality of the food and entertainment. Thirteen days can be a long time if the entertainment is not up to scratch. I am often considered a frustrated entertainer myself, so it was no surprise that I also had a hand in the entertainment. I knew we had to get good entertainment at low cost so we ran a 'Search for a Star' competition in the newspaper. The prize? A free thirteen-night cruise where all they had to do was entertain each night! Later, I would come up with another way to get cheap entertainment, by starting my own entertainment company called The Necessary Steps. I still owe much of the success of my cruises over the years to the many talented entertainers who joined us, including Peter Glen, Frank and Alison Connor, Frank Forde, Dave Butler, Andrew Robley, Denise Latham, Ian Smith and his orchestra, Geoff Taylor, Jayne Sullivan, Paul and Jackie Davis, John Boulter and Anna Dawson, Ruby Murray, Gaynor Connor and Stan Boardman among others. Overall, the first cruise I had chartered was a smashing success, and as we pulled in to Millwall Docks I knew that I belonged on a ship and not in a newspaper office. Plus, I had made a packet – very easily, I considered. You should have seen the look on the faces of my journalist colleagues when I pulled into the company car park in my brand-new Rolls Royce Silver Shadow. I've not been without a Rolls or a Bentley since.

Don't get me wrong, I was still an enthusiastic journalist and I still cared deeply about our newspaper group, but events were overtaking me. My enthusiasm for writing about football began to wane after the 1970 World Cup loss. I was feeling deflated and very restless, so I was happy to hand over the sports writing reigns to Len Whaley,. I'd also already committed myself to two new charters for the following season, while frantically trying to hold together my job as group editor-in-chief. I couldn't have juggled all of my many tasks without Margaret Ryan and John Clarke. On top of my other troubles, people were starting to comment on just how often our newspapers used a picture of the *Black Watch* or the *Blenheim* with an article urging readers to book a cruise arranged especially for them. I needed a new direction to keep getting reader sales, and it came in the form of an incredibly astute businessman and loyal friend called John Batchlor

FOURWINDS

John was one of the most natural and charming sales and marketing experts I have ever met. I got to know him when he was working as a sales rep with Page & Moy, a tour operator that also specialised in reader holidays. It was at first purely a business acquaintanceship, so I was flattered when he invited Jean and me to his wedding in Painswick. After leaving Page & Moy, John formed his own tour operation company in Gloucester and called it, appropriately, Cotsworld Travel. The company specialised in long weekends in that beautiful part of England, along with a few coach trips to the Continent. It just so happened that John was looking for new products to sell and had heard that I had chartered a cruise ship. He was (and still is) a good-humoured, handsome man with a shock of curly blond-brown hair (it's now white), a dapper handlebar moustache and a silver tongue. Not only could he sell ice to eskimos, he would also remember their birthday and send a card. It was no wonder he had such a loyal customer following. In chatting to him at the wedding, we came up with an arrangement whereby I would give him an allocation of cabins on my cruise to sell as a trial. Neither of our lives would ever be the same.

John quickly repeated the success I had achieved with reader offers in Greater London and Essex Newspapers, in newspapers all over the country, including the *Liverpool Echo*, the *Manchester Evening News* and the *Portsmouth Evening News*. Before long, Cotsworld Travel was selling more cruises than I was, and, once again, the ship was full. To thank John and his new wife, Wendy, I invited them on board. Unfortunately (or fortunately as it turned out), John and Wendy couldn't make it and sent in their place John's business partner Alistair Wood and his wife.

"Cotsworld is doing an amazing job selling the reader offer cruises," I enthused over dinner the first night Alistair was on board.

"Yes, we've had some success," he replied, but far from as enthusiastically as I'd expected.

"So how are you finding the travel and tour business up in Gloucester," I asked, somewhat perplexed by his noncommittal comments. "I've found Tel Travel took off running right from the start down in Hornchurch."

"To tell you the truth," Alistair paused, wondering if he should continue his train of thought, "I don't know that this is the right business for me, Terry. We've been very successful with it, as you know, but I've been considering selling my half of the business. I just don't know that I'm cut out for tour operating."

I can't remember exactly what I said to Alistair at the time, but I did see the window of opportunity I had been looking for opening up directly in front of me. Once the cruise finished, I called John and, over lunch and a couple of bottles of wine, I became a 50 per cent shareholder in Cotsworld Travel. As I still had my thriving travel agency in Hornchurch and John's office was in Gloucester, the first decision was where to base the business. I had my heart set on somewhere in Essex, close to home, Jean and the kids, but John was reluctant to move from the Cotswolds.

"Why don't we take a tour of both areas to see what we think," John wisely suggested. Of course, it didn't take long to decide. John drove me around the delightful, quaint villages of Stow-on-the-Wold, Moreton-in-Marsh, Burford and Broadway and, in turn, I took him to Dagenham, Barking, Romford and Basildon. It doesn't take a genius to guess which area we chose. Our new enterprise would be based in Gloucestershire and I would concentrate on the cruise side, while John concentrated on sales. It was another simple decision to make because John was a truly gifted salesman and, before long, the national newspapers were queuing up to run our offers. It certainly helped that John was such a hit with the ladies who looked after the reader offers' section for the provincial and national newspapers. Cruising quickly became the backbone of our business so we decided to concentrate mainly on cruises although land-based holidays still formed an important and profitable part of the business. To become big players in the cruise industry we also needed a more worldly business title. I sold or gave away my share of Tel Travel, Transvan and Emerson Galleries and we bought an ailing company called

Fourwinds Cruises. Newspapers all over the country promoted our cruises and we usually supported them with a promotional evening in a local hotel, where we would show a film of the ship and either John or I would climb on to the stage to give a talk about the wonders of our ship. It was a lucrative public speaking job – some nights we made more money than Frank Sinatra would for a one-night show. We soon turned Fourwinds Cruises into the market leader in cruise charters and in no time at all we had more than 100 office staff and some very prestigious cruise ships were flying the Fourwinds flag. Almost every provincial newspaper group was promoting our cruises and we were soon chartering the *Black Watch*, the *Blenheim* and the *Black Prince* for months at a time. John and I made great business partners; eventually becoming as close as brothers. I could never have enjoyed the success I achieved without him, and I hope he feels the same way. With John as my business partner, my dabbling in chartering cruises was fast becoming a full-time occupation, but I still had loose ends to tidy up. My increasing absences from the office and my newfound passion for cruising was not going unnoticed at the offices of Greater London and Essex Newspapers.

"Valerie, it isn't easy to tell you this," I started out, aware the chairman was not going to be happy to hear that her editor-in-chief was set to sail off into the sunset. "You're all aware that for some time now I have been chartering cruises. Well, the time has come to really give that my best shot, so I thought I'd better come and tell you that I'm going?"

"Where are you going this time, Terry?" It seemed that Valerie didn't really get it. "Madeira?" she asked, confused.

"No, Valerie. I'm sorry but I'm resigning."

"Oh. Are you sure about this, Terry? I mean, have you thought it through? We can look at some options for you if you would like?"

"I'm sorry, Valerie. You know I've enjoyed working here tremendously, but I feel like it's time to move on. John Clarke is extremely capable so I have no doubt he'll fill the role admirably, and of course, I'm prepared to offer him all the support he needs to take over the position before I go."

"Would you consider staying on as a consultant for the group? We'd pay you for your advice, for say three years, and you could help John out in the short term while he finds his feet?"

The board was, in hindsight, very generous and understanding of my situation.

It seemed like an excellent solution. I still got paid, but could concentrate on the cruises full time. Of course, I accepted their offer.

There was no going back and I really applied myself to learning all there was to know about running a cruise ship. I enrolled myself in the Liverpool nautical college and spent countless hours on the bridge every time we sailed in an effort to make up for the fact that I'd come into the industry without going through the usual training regime. I also made sure I understood the economics as well as the technical side of every department on board. There was no room for errors.

THE COTSWOLDS

"How would you feel about moving to the Cotswolds?" I asked Jean over dinner one night.

"No way!" Jean replied, with more than a hint of disapproval in her voice. She'd spent all her life in Essex and her mother and sister still lived there. She was very reluctant to move out of her comfort zone, despite the kids and I having fallen in love with the Cotswolds.

"Well, how about Madeira then? I've decided we should buy that block of land in São Gonçalo and build on it. It's a lovely place, you said so yourself. And it makes sense since all of our cruises are going there and we can fly in and out whenever we like." Things had been going so well for Fourwinds that we chartered a Boeing 757 from Gatwick weekly, flying some of our passengers into Funchal, rather than brave the terrible weather in the Bay of Biscay.

"It'll be a beautiful place for a holiday home," Jean agreed. I did notice the emphasis on the world 'holiday'.

"Perhaps it would be better to buy an apartment in the Cotswolds then," I suggested. "Until we can convince you to move."

"Might have it a long time," Jean answered. And she was right, I still have the apartment I bought at the Cotswold stately home called Brockhampton Park, though I did eventually convince Jean to move. I was sure that the house I was planning in Madeira would lure her away from Essex. It was set to be a stunning Mediterranean-style villa perched high on a hill with panoramic, picturesque views over the whole of Funchal and the harbour. I spared no expense in constructing that house, which was built for me by a friend called Denis Pestana. Denis owned the Carlton and Casino Park

Hotel and was a good friend as well as a successful businessman, building the Pestana Group into one of the biggest hotel groups in the world with more than 800 properties. The house was stunning, including handmade Portuguese tiles, terracotta pathway and drive (and even the double garage), five bedrooms (each also with a terracotta terrace), five bathrooms and even a beautiful apartment for the maid. It was a magnificent house. I even went to the trouble of becoming a Portuguese resident, anticipating the day when it would be our permanent home. There was just one problem. Madeira is renowned for its fantastic climate and was such a popular place for cruising because of the brilliant sunshine, which seemed to flood the island – with the sole exception of our house! At virtually any time of year you could find the island bathed in sunshine, but there was, without exception, always a cold, black cloud sitting right over the top of our house! The only time the cloud wasn't sitting there, it was inside the house itself, making everything damp. Not a day went by when we didn't have a roaring fire going, and we still had mildew growing on our shoes. The conditions were not only frustrating for us; our maid Vera (who the kids ended up nicknaming Vera from Madeira) had a constant job to keep the house clean and damp-free. Meanwhile, down in Funchal they were soaking up the warmth. Denis, being a local, couldn't really see the problem with the lack of sunshine, but as a way around it he suggested I kept the house locked up and used the penthouse suite in the Carlton when I stayed on the island instead – there went the idea of the house in Madeira becoming our family home. Instead, we bought land in the Cotswold town of Winchcombe and set about designing another home – one that would hopefully be much cosier.

TOMATOES, WHAT A NUISANCE!

Luxurious as our home may have been, I was away from it for months at a time. Mind you, no one was complaining, cruising provided our family with a wonderful lifestyle. There was really only one problem – tomatoes. Fred. Olsen cruise ships made most of their money out of importing tomatoes from the Canary Islands on their return voyage. While they acted as ballast and generally made the return voyage much smoother, they proved quite a hassle for the captain and crew. It meant that the fourteenth night of the cruise was always taken up with unloading case after case of tomatoes at Millwall Docks and that we were unable to change our itinerary because we knew there was a shipload of tomatoes waiting to be picked up in the Canaries. As loyal as our regular cruisers were, there was a limit to how many times they wanted to sail from Millwall Docks to Madeira, Lanzarote, Tenerife and Las Palmas. On the rare occasion we were able to squeeze in a cruise to the Mediterranean we jokingly placed a large notice on the bridge. It read: Turn Left At Gibraltar.

The winter months were not the best time to be cruising in the bitterly cold North Atlantic and it made hardy sailors of both our crew and loyal passengers. If it were not for the tomatoes, we would have had the luxury of slowing down or amending our itinerary to avoid the worst storms, but we always knew that there were 100,000 boxes of tomatoes sitting on the quay at Santa Cruz, forcing us to arrive there by Wednesday morning come rain, hail, snow or seasickness. The worst crossing I can ever remember – even more dire than my first cruising experience – occurred where the English Channel meets the notoriously stormy entrance to the infamous Bay of Biscay. It was a charter we did aboard the *Black Prince*, and it illustrated the grave importance of making sure the ship makes contact with big, sometimes 25-metre high waves at the correct angle. On that occasion, even our famed Denny Brown stabilisers were unable to prevent the ship sustaining severe damage when a massive wave crashed through the bridge in the middle of the night, destroying vital controls and impeding our ability to manoeuvre, navigate and communicate with passengers. As you can imagine, in the pitch black the entire experience was terrifying – plunging the passengers and crew into darkness as the Atlantic Ocean boiled and crashed over the bow. Water gushed through a gaping hole, where the bridge windows once were, to infiltrate the ship. The crew, despite their alarm, reacted promptly and calmly and we soon had crew members at their emergency stations throughout the ship to reassure terrified passengers that we were not going to sink. It was certainly a hair-raising few hours, after which the *Black Prince* limped into Plymouth for a timely temporary repair job, which was completed in just three days. Incredibly, for such a frightening experience, many of our passengers weren't put off cruising for life – we had only our crew to thank for that. Passengers were told that, in light of the catastrophe, they could choose to be taken home immediately with a full refund or stay onboard during repairs and accompany the ship on a shortened cruise. Most of them, it turned out, where happy to remain on board. Of course, as with any such serious incident at sea, an investigation into our handling of the crisis was ordered. Our crew had reacted admirably in my opinion, but we were still keen to ensure that everyone had done their utmost to reassure passengers.

During the investigation, it was brought to my attention that one elderly lady had fainted on the staircase. The woman was one of those who had chosen to remain on board, so I thought I would take the chance to talk to her in person to find out why she had been so afraid.

"What was it that scared you so much," I asked her.

"Well, your pianist Steve was standing at the top of the stairs in his pyjamas talking to passengers through a loud hailer," she informed me. "I went closer so I could hear what he was saying and suddenly…I noticed his pyjamas were wide open at the front. He was showing everything – I just fainted at the sight of it!"

Pianist indeed!

Of course, as was usually the case on the Fred.Olsen cruises to the Canaries, once we reached Cape Finisterre, the sun broke through the clouds and all bad weather was quickly forgotten. It helped that our standards were exceptionally high, especially when it came to catering and entertainment. It meant that, weather aside, our passengers always enjoyed themselves. Those that did not, particularly on the *Blenheim*, were sometimes in for a surprise. Captain David Smethurst, as mentioned, had a very dry sense of humour but was also rather stubborn – another trait that fulfilled the Yorkshireman typecast. Like every business, despite best efforts to please and appease passengers, there are always a few whose complaints or requests are entirely unreasonable. A few such passengers must rue the day they ever met Captain David Smethurst. On a few occasions (very few I must admit), crew members would be beset with unjustified complaints that they would take to the captain, inevitably finishing with, "They've asked to see you, Captain Smethurst."

"Tell them I'm busy and I'll meet with them at Madeira," Captain Smethurst would, rather unorthodoxly, reply. On arriving at Madeira, those who had not relaxed and settled into ship life would finally be granted an audience with the captain, who did his best to smooth their ruffled feathers. However, if a compromise was unable to be reached, it was very likely that the unhappy passenger's cruise would end there and then. Captain Smethurst did kick some unreasonable guests off the ship at Madeira – problem solved! Aside from those few obnoxious customers, the major frustration with the Fred.Olsen cruise ships remained the tomatoes, and John Batchlor and I were getting increasingly concerned about putting all of our eggs (or tomatoes) in one basket. As it turned out, Fred.Olsen lines were also reassessing their options. The tomato contract was drawing to an end, and when young Frederick Olsen took over the reins of the company from the four Fred Olsens who had preceded him he had new and different ideas on its direction. A decision was made to sell the *Black Watch* and the *Blenheim* and to convert the *Black Prince* into a cruise-only vessel. Eventually the *Blenheim* was sold to an American company, who used it for short cruises out of Miami until the time came for the old girl to retire. She retired in a way that many grand old ships did in those days – with a fire that led to a huge insurance payout. The *Black Watch* was sold to a different buyer and renamed *Jupiter*. John and I continued to charter it as a Fourwinds cruise ship for some years. The *Black Prince*, I am happy to say, went on for many successful years before losing some of her dignity when she was sold as a ferry to a company in Venezuela in 2009. The end of our affiliation with Fred.Olsen lines, however, presented us with another challenge – it meant we desperately needed more cruise ships to pull into the Fourwinds stable. Cue another man who would change my life.

STUPID ENGLISHMAN!

"Hello, I am here to meet with a Mr Lewis, could you please show me to his table?" I asked the Maître d', as I strode confidently into London's Savoy Hotel.

"I am sorry, I don't have any table booked under that name," the Maître d' answered, after a quick scan of his reservations' book.

"Oh, really? A Mr George Lewis? It was definitely a booking made for lunch at 1 pm today. Could you please check again?"

"I am sorry, Sir. I definitely don't have anyone booked under that name."

"Can you please try Zarponelli for me then? Nothing booked under Aris Zarponelli?"

"I'm afraid not, sir," he answered, rather curtly this time, after again checking his reservations diary. There must be a mistake, I thought as I made my way to the bar. I waited at the bar for a good 15 minutes, but I was a busy man and eventually there was nothing for it but to head home. As soon as I stepped in the door, I received a call from Aris Zarponelli. Aris was our mutual contact, himself a big player in the shipping industry.

"Terry, where on earth are you? George is here and we've been waiting for more than half an hour. He is a very busy man, Terry, as you know. Are you on your way?"

"On my way? Aris, I arrived there at precisely 1 pm and waited until about quarter past but was told that there was no table booked today for Lewis or for Zarponelli."

"Lewis?" Aris queried.

"Yes, I asked to be directed to George Lewis's table and they told me they did not have a booking."

"That is because it is Louris, Terry. L.O.U.R.I.S. George Louris. Are you able to turn around and come back now?'" Aris sounded slightly exasperated. To be perfectly honest, turning around and going back to lunch was just about the last thing I wanted to do and my nose was a little out of joint. This Mr Louris might be a very important and busy man, but so was I! Aris was a good contact and friend, that was for sure, and would go on to become a vice president of Silverseas Cruises, but I had the distinct feeling that I was wasting my time on this meeting. As it turned out, that could not have been further from the truth.

"Terry, nice of you to join us," George Louris smiled and raised a long, slim finger from the table, more for the purpose of ashing his cigarette than in recognition of my presence. He was the perfect image of a Greek shipping magnate – suave, swarthy and dressed impeccably in an expensive cream linen suit and handmade crocodile-skin shoes. Ice chinked in his glass of whiskey as he raised his drink in a further gesture of welcome. I noted the diamond cufflinks in his pristine white shirt cuffs. My immediate impression of him, as I watched him slip a £20 note into the top pocket of the head waiter, was one of dislike. Whatever my initial thoughts on the man, however, he had certainly done his homework on me. I was soon to find that not only were my first impressions misleading, but that we would embark on a business partnership that was to earn us both a fortune – and send my hair from black to white! George Louris was certainly supremely confident, dominating the conversation as well as the grill room of the Savoy for the duration of our meeting. He smoothed his shiny black hair with his hand as he began, speaking with that breathy directness common to Greeks.

"I have studied the way you operate the Fred.Olsen ships," he paused to flick his cigarette, somewhat arrogantly it seemed to me, "…and I am impressed…very impressed. Now, I would like you to become commodore of my company. I would like you to help establish a cruise ship on the English market."

My reaction was instinctive and just as direct. "Thank you, but I am very happy doing what I am doing now."

His dark eyes caught mine and he instinctively raised an eyebrow, a small, slightly scathing smile played around his lips. He had the somewhat patronising demeanour of a cat toying with a mouse.

"Stupid Englishman," this endearment, which I was to hear many times over the next few years, was accompanied by a wry smile and another dismissive flick of the cigarette. "Only an Englishman would turn down a proposition before he has heard it. Please allow me the courtesy to explain the proposition before you say no."

Of course, he was correct. I had dismissed him out of hand without considering or even listening to his offer. George and his partner, Angelo Lenardartis, owned a cruise line called Intercruise and the pride of their fleet was a vessel called *La Palma*. In its former incantation of *La Perla* the ship had a chequered history operating week-long cruises out of Venice during summer but hardly being used for much of the year. George's plan was to reinvent the ship as *La Palma* and operate it out of the UK when it was not being used for cruises from Venice.

"As commodore, you have complete authority on the ship's operation – even above me," he explained. "And I would pay you very well for the honour of being my commodore."

"Thank you, but I already do quite well for myself with Fourwinds," I commented.

"One thousand pounds, no?" he queried, with a touch of pride in his voice. "One thousand pounds – per day, you earn?" George Louris asked, knowing that it was unlikely I earned anywhere near that extraordinary amount. "Three hundred and sixty-five thousand pounds a year I pay you, my friend."

Not surprisingly, after a quick consultation with John, we decided it was too good an opportunity to pass up. My £1000 a day 'wage' would be deducted from the cost of our own charters. I headed home to pack for Venice.

LA PALMA

Two immaculate stewards collected me from the Venice airport on a beautiful, sunny spring day and then ferried me by motor launch to Stazione Maritima, where I had my first glimpse of *La Palma*. Against the glimmering backdrop of the lagoon, St Mark's Square and the Doge's Palace, the vessel certainly looked magnificent. The ship was immaculate in gleaming white, emblazoned with the Intercruise logo on its blue funnel. Matching blue canvas sunshades covered the expansive decks and a team of hostesses wearing Greek national costume were handing ice-cold, fresh orange juice to embarking passengers. A line of senior officers stood, military style, on the quayside to welcome me (some of them would soon be disembarking…permanently, but of course they were not yet to know that). On board, George stood with his family, beaming proudly. He was obviously extremely proud of the ship, pointing out its features as we stood side-by-side on the bridge while the ship sailed elegantly past the Bridge of Sighs en route for our first port of call, Athens. George was nothing if not an attentive, courteous and loyal friend to me (sometimes too loyal, as you will later discover) but I did notice that the Greek officers on the bridge, to a man, looked terrified of him as he spoke sharply to them in guttural Greek.

My cabin was opulent to say the least. George had it prepared for me personally and I was welcomed to my quarters by my own personal steward, Manolis, who was to serve me faithfully for many years. As soon as I stepped inside it took my breath away. Marble and polished mahogany adorned my day cabin and contrasted with the white leather furnishings. It contained a personal galley, a polished mahogany desk (from which I could electronically control my personal TV aerial, which had been installed at the highest point of the mast) and, off to one side, Manolis' quarters. Huge double doors led to my night cabin, which featured a comfortable king-size bed and a breathtaking marble bathroom. It was certainly luxurious – if only the passengers' accommodation had been of a similar standard!

The *La Palma*, when I first boarded her, featured the kind of class divisions that could only lead, in my opinion, to a full-blown passenger riot. Not only were the passengers' cabins far less elegant than my own, if not downright sub-standard, but the ship was not renowned for the quality of its food and it did not take me long to figure out why. As the passengers queued patiently for a meagre fare of an awful lot of salads coupled with cheap processed meats and fish, followed by some sad-looking cakes, they were able to look out at the sun deck where George had his own personal table. The food being served at the buffet table inside certainly paled in significance to that set out as George's fare. A whole fresh lobster, crabs, steaks and chops, and a perfectly grilled giant sea bass, all graced the centre of George's table. His philosophy was simple but far from egalitarian – he and the senior officers had the first share of the spoils, followed by the crew and their families, and then what was left would be offered to the passengers. Clearly, I had a lot of work to do. My initial tour of the ship revealed much that was depressing, but *La Palma* had enough potential to convince me that we could easily create the standards and atmosphere Fourwinds' passengers expected. Its benefits included plentiful deck space – certainly more than that on the Fred.Olsen ships – as well as a wonderful promenade deck that could be covered in glass in to create sunny winter lounges. From a layout perspective, it was a beautiful ship because its expansive deck space meant that it never looked too crowded, but never seemed too empty either. The show lounge lent itself to some spectacular entertainment, but, above all else, *La Palma* could take 800 passengers at a time on a very low daily running cost – statistics I knew could make us very rich. On the downside, the galley needed to be gutted and entirely rebuilt to meet the hygiene standards I (and the British health authorities) required. We would also need to furnish the ship with some more luxurious suites. The suites in the passenger quarters were simply slightly larger cabins with fitted carpet that climbed the walls, hiding a multitude of sins. George never really understood the need for more luxurious cabins on the lower decks. Although he never objected to the amount of money spent on refurbishment, he was a little perplexed by my concern for the lower-class passengers. He never went down to the passenger accommodation and, although he authorised the construction of beautiful suites on the sun deck and promenade deck, as you descended to the cheaper cabins the décor became decidedly dodgy.

"I really think we need to renovate the cabins on the lower decks," I insisted.

"What for? You should just persuade them to book a more expensive cabin." George would argue.

"There's a lot that needs to be done, George. Are you sure you're prepared to undertake such extensive renovations?"

"Whatever you need, Commodore." True to his word, he casually waved away any concerns I had about the amount of money that needed to be spent on the ship before we set sail for the UK in November. Few of the repairs required to upgrade the ship could be done at sea, so most were scheduled during the two-month lay-up at the end of the summer season.

"We'll take the necessary steps," George assured me, shaking my hand and faithfully promising both the funds and the contacts to get the repairs done in the dock at Piraeus at the end of the season. The 'necessary steps' was one of George's trademark phrases and would later be the name bestowed on our onboard entertainment company.

I spent most of that summer aboard *La Palma*, fastidiously checking every detail, down to the last rivet, with the help and advice of John Pavlou, the senior engineer, and the young Greek captain Christos Christofiordis. Although the captain was a great hit with the passengers, unfortunately he lacked the experience of sailing the tempestuous North Atlantic in winter, so he was the first to be replaced. The mainly Greek crew were fine, for the most part, but to run cruises successfully from the UK my experience told me that passengers preferred a proportion of British officers and a higher percentage of British crew. In my view, the British were always the best from a technical point of view, but while I would choose British officers over other nationality any day, British table stewards and cabin stewards were a nightmare. Generally, the most professional catering and cabin staff were Portuguese; however, if the passengers were tipping well the Greeks and Italians could be first class as well. The Greek crew always knew how to get the biggest tips from passengers, and, when added to the inevitable fiddles that went on, they always did very well for themselves. All of them had jobs they didn't want to lose. However, few of the officers had the experience I felt was necessary, so I decided to replace them all with officers that had the experience of command in the North Atlantic. This meant that each of our officers of the watch was an experienced captain in his own right and, under the command of Captain Nick Papathanasiou, one of the most experienced masters in the world, I knew our passengers could feel secure. I personally interviewed Nick for the job and explained the set up to him in detail. But he was never happy at having to play second fiddle to me and from very positive beginnings our relationship gradually soured. After a couple of years, I felt I had no option but to replace him. I may have had less sailing experience than Nick, but when it came to running a cruise ship, I certainly knew more than he did, and often proved it, which must have irritated him at times.

La Palma was lucky to have such an experienced crew and equally as lucky to have such an excellent engineering team, under the leadership of superintendent engineer John Pavlou. In all our years of sailing *La Palma*, she was never late arriving at a port of call due to a technical or engineering breakdown – a record the *Queen Elizabeth II* could never boast. On several occasions that I can recall, we passed that ship as it limped along with some mechanical failure or other.

All through the summer of 1985, *La Palma* hosted a series of seven-night cruises from Venice, sailing via the Corinth Canal to Athens, Rhodes, Crete, Corfu and Dubrovnik. While on board, I set about reinventing the personality of the ship, starting with the entertainment and the catering. To complete the new British makeover we had to redesign the casino and shops and bring on our own team of photographers. I organised these as straightforward concessions. Concessionaires were charged £1 per passenger per day and any profit above that was theirs. An old mate of mine, Graham McCallion, was a top-notch photographer, so I loaned him the money to purchase his photographic equipment and set up his business on board. It was another situation that benefited everyone – Graham and his wife Sue, our passengers, and me.

Given that hairdressing was almost a family tradition for the Hopleys, we decided to run the salon ourselves.

Frank and Alison Connor, two of my old ship-mates from the Fred. Olsen days, were the perfect pair to organise the entertainment. With them as partners, we formed the aforementioned entertainment company The Necessary Steps. It was a big success and I can never thank them enough for the professional way they set about organising musicians, dancers, singers, specialitty acts and cruise staff for *La Palma* and Fourwinds cruises, as well as excelling at creating dazzling costumes, sets and arrangements. All of the entertainment, down to the most minute detail, was organised by the team. Alison would buy the material for the elaborate costumes and commandeer a pavilion at her parents' home as a temporary workshop while her team set about creating a visual masterpiece. Dancers were recruited and rehearsals began well before the cruise season started, taking place in a local church hall until we boarded the ship. I am proud to say that we never had a cabaret artist just walk on stage and do a 45-minute stint, the way many modern cruise ships do. We always had a spectacular show with dancing girls in exquisite costumes, unique musical arrangements and an elaborate main act of theatre, music or comedy. Our shows left those of our competitors' for dust. As a result of our entertainment staff's incredible efforts, my 'welcome aboard' speech always informed passengers: "Quite simply, we have the best entertainment of any ship afloat. I will ask you if you agree with me on the last night of the cruise." On the final night of every cruise when I asked that question, I always received a deafening roar of approval.

However, life on board ship was not all about entertainment, I also needed to sort out more practical matters, such as a medical centre. I always found it difficult to get good medical staff on cruise ships. Eventually we decided that rather than make it a permanent posting, we would gather a panel of GPs, with each prepared to take on the job for a month or two-month contract. They would become the ship's doctor during that time in return for a free cruise for themselves and their families. Once again, my staff came to my rescue and I was helped out by Dr Nick Stoy and his wife Liz, who put together a panel of doctors for when Dr Stoy was unable to sail. Dr Stoy became one of the great characters on board and I owe him for a lot more than that. He was also the man who sorted out one of my most painful and pressing problems – the slipped disc that had been making my life a misery for many years. I had injured my back in my twenties while playing tennis, and was sometimes confined to bed for weeks. I'd even had a plaster of Paris corset from chest to hips for a while. Of course, like all back injuries, it flared up at the most inappropriate times and this was one of them. Maybe it was my intense involvement in running all aspects of *La Palma* that brought it on, but my back pain had reached a fever pitch and I could often be found, unable to sleep, wandering the decks at night literally dragging one leg behind me. One day on the bridge I mentioned to Dr Stoy that I was thinking of having a laminectomy, an orthopaedic procedure that involved fusing together the discs in my back. It would put me on my back for six weeks and require a further six months of recovery, and that was if I was lucky.

"Please Terry," Dr Stoy cautioned, "before you consider doing that you really must see a colleague of mine. He's a neurosurgeon, Mr Henry Marsh, who works at Atkinson Morley Hospital in Wimbledon."

I trusted Dr Stoy implicitly and duly visited Henry Marsh in London's south-west.

"Have you heard of a procedure called a micro-discectomy?" Mr Marsh enquired, after having assessed my problem. I hadn't.

"Well it takes less than an hour, so you would only need to be hospitalised for a couple of days and you could be back on board in less than two weeks," he told me. I immediately agreed to go ahead. It was, in my opinion, nothing short of a miracle. When I entered hospital, it was with an excruciating pain running down my left leg. Three days later, I left hospital with an incision that was less than one inch long and with no pain whatsoever. The operation was such a success that, fifteen years later, when a disc higher up my spine began to give me trouble, I went straight back in and had another operation. Decades later my back causes me pain from time to time, but nothing like that which I used to suffer.

In our family, back pain was not only confined to me. Our beautiful daughter Michelle was diagnosed with scoliosis while she was still at school. Her twisted spine had to be corrected by an uncomfortable and sometimes agonising back brace. She never knew it, but I often sat by her beside at night and wept when I saw her in that terrible straightjacket. I was terrified that her condition would worsen. True to her nature, my loving little girl never once complained about it, but I felt her pain and it hurt me more than my back problems ever had. Although her condition did not deteriorate, it didn't improve much either, but today Michelle carries herself with such grace that only her closest family and friends can spot her scoliosis. As always, she made up for this difficulty with her vivacious personality. She was a true chatterbox as a little girl, immediately introducing herself to any house guests and conversing as if she were an adult herself. Before long she would be holding court and dominating the conversation until we politely excused her and packed her off to bed. She also considered herself to be my little assistant, accompanying me whenever she could in my early days as a journalist and playing a key sales role when we moved into the cruise industry. Later, when she was a bit older, Michelle knew everything and everyone on board ship. Even as commodore I knew if I wanted to find out anything about any of the staff on board, I only had to ask my daughter. She also proved herself extremely capable at whatever she turned her hand to and she definitely inherited my work ethic. Her sales experience was honed at Emerson Galleries, where she one day sold a gorgeous dining suite to a delighted middle-aged couple, only to skip off later in the evening to her work at Cotsworld Travel. Imagine the aforesaid couple's surprise when they stopped into a travel agency later in the evening to book a cruise and found the same charming and knowledgeable sales girl, who was then able to tell them all they wanted to know about cruising. That's Michelle for you.

As a child, my son Terry was certainly a different kettle of fish. He was a mad keen sportsman with an enthusiasm for the outdoor life, but was not one bit interested in academic studies. I modelled my parenting on my own dad, who was a strict disciplinarian with his children but still the most loving father you could ever meet. I was certainly harder on Terry than I ever was on any of my staff on board ship. As a very young child, Terry had a fascinating sense of logic. His reasoning made perfect sense to him, but left the rest of us wondering. One morning I had to take our dog, an excitable boxer named Jane, to the family vet.

"Can I come, daddy?" Five-year-old Terry pleaded.

"Come on then. Put your shoes on," I hurried him up, with Jane straining at the leash and none the wiser.

"Why do we have to go to the vet?" my son queried.

"Because the vet needs to give Jane an injection."

"What's a vet?"

"It's a dog's doctor," I explained, putting it to him as simply as possible.

Terry went quiet and said nothing. When he sat down in the antiseptic-smelling waiting room, where a number of other canine patients were cowering beneath chairs or trembling in their owner's arms, he looked confused. He carefully eyeballed the cocker spaniel, alsatian and labrador that were awaiting their turn to go in.

"Which one is the doctor?" he asked.

His childlike sense of logic told him that the dog's doctor would be a dog – and why not!

During Terry's school years, I nearly adopted his grandmother's favourite saying – "Whatever's going to become of us?". As I said, he was a talented sportsman, playing centre forward for the Romford Juniors and I attended many of his games, cheering him on from the sideline and gradually developing strong friendships with the parents of the other players, particularly Trevor and Carol Brown, the parents of Terry's goalkeeper friend Michael. Every year the team and associated parents and friends would take a tour to the continent, where the boys would play local clubs. The tours were always hilarious because the emphasis would be on booking the cheapest accommodation possible in resorts such as Benidorm and Majorca, where we could enjoy a week's full board for just thirty quid each. The boys enjoyed playing local teams, but their real fun came off the pitch in questionable hotels like the Titanic and the Kontiki. Despite my support of his football, I did secretly worry about his prospects once he left school and my worry was far from assuaged when I found out what he had planned.

"I thought I might do an apprenticeship as a plumber," he told me. I groaned inwardly, knowing that this career path was going to be a hard slog. Jean and I were far from thrilled by his choice and gave him no assistance of any kind. There was often a tear in our eyes as we watched our boy trudge off to the station in the biting cold at 6 am. Thankfully, it was not long before Terry realised that there had to be other, better ways of making a living.

"Why don't you come aboard the *Black Watch*? You can start out selling tours and excursions." I was secretly pleased that the plumbing had not worked out and that my son might now follow me into a career at sea, but the position I offered was still very junior. I knew it was important that my kids adopted the strong work ethic Jean and I had been raised with, and I am pleased to say that they both have. "The record for onboard sales for tours before we reach Madeira is £20,000. Let's see how you go topping that," I grinned. I was taking a few days off and thought it might be fun to set him a rather hefty, though achievable, target in his little excursions office. Three days later, I was standing on the quay waiting for the ship as it berthed in Madeira. As I gazed up at the bridge I saw a tousled blonde head poke out. Terry was hanging out over the side.

"Twenty-eight grand!" he yelled, with all the passengers looking on.

"Shhh," I placed my finger on my lips, but I could hardly keep the grin from spreading across my face. From then on, Terry never looked back.

A RECIPE FOR DISASTER

Terry's success in the shore excursions office was encouraging, but there was one department that was almost to be my son's downfall (and my own!) – the catering department. In my opinion, few divisions are as vital to the success of a cruise ship as the catering division, but ours almost put *La Palma* out of business before we even began. The fault was entirely mine. I had appointed an old friend of mine, who shall remain nameless, to the position of chief catering officer. I suppose you could say that I let our friendship cloud my judgement of his experience and ability, but I was to learn my lesson. It isn't easy for a catering officer to sink a big cruise ship, but that is exactly what he almost did!

Just as we had for the entertainment, we created a new company to manage the catering and bars on board. The company was named Ocean Leisure Overseas Ltd and I (foolishly in retrospect) gave my friend and new chief catering officer a 50 per cent share in the company. The other 50 per cent I gave to Terry. I was certainly placing a lot of trust in my friend and Terry sure did learn a lot – about how NOT to do it! During the first summer aboard *La Palma*, while I was checking technical details our new chief catering officer was checking out the ship's catering areas. He decreed that he needed not only a new galley but also new cold storage and dry storage areas. George often raised an eyebrow, but never complained about the amount of money he was being asked to spend and *La Palma* was soon fitted with a top-of-the-range new galley complete with a brand new bakery. Under the watchful eyes of the Greek provisions master, Dimitris, the storage areas were also redesigned and fitted. The first cruise of *La Palma*, flying the Fourwinds flag, was a positioning cruise sailing out of Athens to Plymouth, England, which was to be our home port. Plymouth's location on the south-west coast saved us two day's sailing compared to London and allowed us to fit Agadir or Casablanca into our winter Canary Islands schedule. Hindsight is a wonderful thing, and when I think of it now I wish we had sailed to Plymouth empty, as a shakedown cruise to give the new crew time to settle. But we didn't. We had, of course, conducted successful sea trials in the Aegean, with most of our new crew on board, weeks in advance of the cruise's scheduled start. Our new English staff flew out to join the ship a week before we were set to sail. The ship was buzzing with the hubbub of dancers and musicians rehearsing almost non-stop and the shops, hairdressers, and croupiers were busily preparing for a perfect maiden voyage. The hospital was staffed and equipped, the engineers were working ceaselessly in the stifling engine room and the twenty-seven chefs prepared their menus and scrubbed the galley until it gleamed. On the bridge, the officers were making themselves familiar with our brand-new radars and navigation systems. There was only one thing missing – food!

"Sorry Terry. It seems I got the dates wrong," the chief catering officer informed me when I enquired as to why there was literally no food on board for the crew.

"Don't worry, everything will be here before the passengers."

But I was worried! Can you imagine the logistics, and the expense, of having to send 300 crew members ashore three times a day to eat? By now, George was convinced that our new man in charge of catering was a professional saboteur. Thankfully, George had decided to come to the rescue himself and used his own contacts to victual the ship. It meant that, against all our plans, we would be serving a very Greek menu on our first unforgettable voyage.

"I know it was a stuff up, but it was just a technical hitch," my friend pleaded with me. "A few problems getting English food to Athens. It'll all be fine when we get to Plymouth," he argued. I was far from convinced, but there wasn't really time to rectify the problem as passengers were due to arrive within days.

"Terry, I think our passengers…would like a new jewellers on board?" George's approach was given away by the tinkling of ice, as he was rarely seen on board without a glass of whiskey on the rocks. As a renowned party animal, he often also carried around a small shot glass, which he used to flush out his red-rimmed, jaundiced eyes after a big night in his cabin entertaining. To compound my problems, George was hell bent on installing new shops – now, at the eleventh hour!

"But passengers are due to arrive tomorrow. And the builders are still working on the cabins. I just cannot see how it can be done, George. Can't it wait until next time?" I argued.

"No, no. It will be fine. I will take the necessary steps and we will build a beautiful new jewellers. And, I think, a new duty-free shop, Terry. Yes, yes, a new duty-free shop!" George grinned his most charming smile. I was secretly despairing, but it was his ship. Soon carpenters, plumbers and decorators, all of whom had been busily putting finishing touches to our new passenger cabins and luxury suites, were whisked off to build George's new shops. To their credit – and my astonishment! – they did manage to put in a new jewellers and duty-free shop in a 24-hour period; however, it also meant that the new paint in the cabins was not yet dry and new toilets were still being installed as the first planeloads of passengers touched down in Athens.

"Welcome to Athens," our reception team told our passengers at the airport. "'As a special bonus we are going to take you on a tour of the Acropolis and Parthenon before we board *La Palma.*"

Most of the passengers were tired and not impressed with their surprise three-hour tour, designed solely to give enough time for paint and varnish to dry and the last of the carpet to be laid. Just minutes before the first passengers boarded the ship, the denims came off and the officers reappeared, immaculate in their uniforms and the perfect vision of order and control, with no indication of the pandemonium of the previous 24 hours. It was an amazing recovery. Incredibly, despite being served rhubarb leaves as a vegetable and Yorkshire pudding that resembled the sole of a workman's boot, both in taste and appearance (our Greek chefs having not yet come to grips with the finer points of English cuisine), our passengers appeared to be having a good time. The ship behaved impeccably as we sailed to Malta, Sardinia, Malaga, Majorca, Gibraltar, Lisbon and on to Millbay Docks, Plymouth. Interestingly, our new chief catering officer was nowhere to be found at several critical times on the cruise. I never did discover where he hid himself.

When we landed in Plymouth, we had just 24 hours to re-provision and prepare ourselves for the first of six two-week cruises to Lisbon, Madeira,

Tenerife, Lanzarote, Las Palmas and Casablanca. It was a rainy, cold November and the weather forecast was ominous. Luckily, despite the elements, all the cruises were a complete sell out, but my troubles were just beginning. A line of trucks were queued at the docks, waiting for our arrival. Because we were a new venture, when we landed in Plymouth we had to take on a great deal of things, including fuel, fresh water, new linen, furniture, curtains, musical instruments, sound equipment and lighting. On top of that, of course, we needed enough provisions for a two-week cruise, as well as a 10 per cent margin. It was a huge amount to have to load and organise, made doubly difficult by the over-enthusiastic ordering of our chief catering officer.

"Commodore, I need you urgently," Port Captain John Willan rushed up to the bridge, concern written all over his ruddy face. "You have more supplies out there than the British Army took to the bloody Falklands!" he explained, as he wiped at the sweat that had begun beading his forehead. As far as the eye could see, lorries stretched along the docks, but I had not been aware they were blocking off half of Plymouth as well! Trucks carrying meat, fruit and vegetables, eggs, wine, tea, coffee, milk and all manner of delicacies were bumper to bumper, and the drivers were starting to get irate. For the first time in my life, I had no idea what to do. Not a clue!

"For Christ's sake, get the junior catering staff together," I urged my son Terry.

"Take on as much as possible and what you think you need. The rest we will just have to turn away. Give it away if you have to."

Of course, the truck drivers were none too pleased about having to wait for the surplus to be loaded and about some of it not being taken. It was a nightmare.

"Mate, it's not my fault. I ordered the correct amount. We don't have enough storage space on board," my friend the chief catering officer insisted, scratching his head every time we refused yet another juggernaut full of coffee. We took on as much as we could. Soon the ship's halls and alleyways were stacked to the brim with provisions and we even drained the swimming pool so we could stack it with cases of baked beans and tinned tomatoes.

"Commodore, I can't get into my cabin," the Greek hotel manager soon informed me. It was floor to ceiling full of egg crates and just one slip would have them tumbling down. Later, we would discover that we had so many eggs that even if every man, woman and child had eaten sixteen eggs a day and washed each one down with a bottle of wine, we would still have not made a dent in the supply of those two products on that cruise!

"What about all those kegs of beer," Port Captain Willan pointed. It was the last straw.

"We can't even serve bloody beer on tap on board!" I groaned, feeling sick to my stomach. "And there must be at least 100 kegs there!"

Sure enough, a well-known brewery had unloaded 100 kegs of draught beer on the quayside.

"No worries, Commodore, I'll get a crane driver to help put those kegs up on deck ten," my now ex-friend informed me.

"You can't be serious," I spat. "The topmost deck? The bloody ship'll capsize if we put anything up there at funnel height."

"Don't even think about it," the chief engineer agreed, "or we'll turn over as soon as the first wave hits us."

"We'll just have to leave them behind. Give the damn things away if necessary," I instructed, seething. The weather outside the harbour was deteriorating and we were by now several hours behind schedule. By 10 pm – a mere five hours late – we were (more than) fully provisioned and ready to sail, until an officer who had been undertaking a security check came running up to me.

"Commodore, deck ten is stacked with heavy barrels of beer. It's a disaster."

"What the...? Where the hell is the chief catering officer!"

I stormed up to deck ten where, sure enough, our illustrious chief catering officer had bribed a crane drive to stack up the beer barrels. There they were – useless to us as we could not serve beer on tap – stacked in the most vulnerable part of the ship in the hope that no one would go up there before we set sail. It was ludicrous and extremely dangerous. Of course, by that stage we couldn't find a crane driver to remove the kegs, so we had to delay sailing yet again while the poor crew physically manhandled the heavy kegs off the ship. It was the worst day of my cruising career and I take full responsibility for employing the man in the first place. Fourwinds undertook a complete inquest, during which we realised that some of the supplies ordered for the two-week cruise would have lasted the ship at least seven years! However, my friend still refused to concede he had made a mistake and even had the temerity to sue me for wrongful dismissal when I fired him. It took a long, expensive legal battle before the truth of his incompetence came out. That was one of the downsides of British staff: unlike the Greeks or Portuguese, they were highly unionised. Such was the power of the unions at that time that it was almost impossible to fire any British staff members, no matter how incompetent they were. It certainly wasn't like that on other ships. If someone was no good, they were thrown off, as simple as that. It meant that they knew they had to do their job properly, so they usually did and very rarely were people fired.

On a positive note following the catering debacle I realised things could only get better. We never had that kind of stuff-up on *La Palma* again, but things were still a little rocky in our first winter cruising season out of Plymouth. Storm after storm besieged us that first winter, but I had literally crawled all over the keel to make sure *La Palma* was strong and she didn't let us down. We also had the luxury of being able to divert the ship to Porto, Lisbon or Gibraltar if the crashing waves got too much. By that stage most passengers were so overcome with seasickness they were simply happy to be rid of the bad weather and didn't mind the diversion. It was more of a problem when Plymouth experienced foul weather. Announcing a delay because of sea conditions almost invariably upset passengers, some of whom would march up to the purser's office demanding compensation. Yet, if we did set sail in bad weather, those same passengers would be the first to blame us for putting their lives at risk by venturing out into a force ten. You couldn't win.

On one occasion, we pulled back into Plymouth to find TV vans and arch lights awaiting our return from a particularly bumpy cruise.

"Must be a celebrity joining our next cruise," I thought, little realising it was me the TV reporters wanted to interview.

"Commodore Hopley, why did you put your passengers lives at risk by heading into such a big storm when you left Plymouth two weeks ago?"

It turned out one of our passengers had telephoned the BBC, while safe in Madeira, to complain that passengers' lives were placed at risk by my decision to sail out into a certain storm.

"There was a bit of a swell out there," I informed the reporter in my smoothest voice. "In fact, we delayed sailing until the worst of the weather had passed and we only sailed from Plymouth after the tiny Brittany Ferries had already ventured into the same stretch of ocean."

"That may be the case, but we are told a passenger was seriously hurt by a gaming machine hurtling across the room." He was not going to be placated that easily.

"One of our small one-armed bandits slid off the wall and hit a lady on the arm," I replied. "The doctor told me she had a small bruise."

"We were told the ship was pitching to such a degree that the majority of passengers were absolutely terrified." He still did not want to give up.

"I have been cruising in the North Atlantic for many years," I threw back at him, "and the sea state was moderate to high. Ships sail in far worse conditions every day. If passengers were terrified, I would expect some of them to leave the ship at the first port of call. None did."

Thankfully, the interview was then concluded and we escaped without adverse publicity that might damage future bookings. However, I did feel sympathetic for first-time cruisers who, like me, were probably horrified by their first experience of the volatile North Atlantic in winter, the most treacherous stretch of ocean on the planet.

THE NEEDLES CLUB

Despite excessive catering and the sometimes inclement weather, our first season's sailing was a huge success. We had a wonderful crew, excellent occupancy figures and a well-deserved reputation. As we sailed into Plymouth for the last time that season, I heard the strains of music coming from the crew mess below and went down to investigate. Cheers and applause greeted me. The entire crew had organised a small party to celebrate our success.

"As a token of our appreciation, we'd like you to have this small gift…" I was deeply touched. The officers, staff and crew had pitched in to have one of the onboard jewellers make a 22-carat gold bracelet that was a direct replica of the anchor chain. They even had it engraved. I still treasure that memento today.

As planned, at the end of that first season we spent six weeks cruising in the Norwegian Fjords and then headed off to Venice – our summer home port – via Lisbon, Gibraltar, Malaga, Palma, Nice, Corsica, Sicily, Naples, Rome, Corfu and Dubrovnik. As a bonus for our passengers, they had the choice of returning home aboard the Orient Express or by Concorde. The cruise was an enormous success. Our marketing edge was guaranteed by the inclusion of such lavish and appealing return transport. In fact, I believe Fourwinds became the only company to charter two Concordes and obtain permission for them to take off simultaneously – a spectacle that brought us excellent publicity.

George was thrilled with *La Palma*'s initial success and loved to be onboard. His personal suite was just as elegant and sophisticated as my own, but, unlike mine, it very often contained un-chaperoned ladies, whom George was adamant would be beguiled by his charm and the offer of fish soup at 3 am.

"You really think that's going to work, George?" I often teased him. "Maybe that works with Greek women, but these are Englishwomen. I don't think they're after your fish soup."

Of course, George was a married man with a grown-up family, but that didn't seem to curb his wandering eye. He was a good-looking, charming rogue and despite it taking him some time to realise that the fish soup routine was probably a bit off-putting, he did seem to enjoy a measure of success. Of course, the antics that regularly occurred in George's cabin were absent from mine, but that didn't stop George delightedly pointing out that my cabin wardrobe, like his, was equipped with a cunningly conceived 'escape door' that led out to the promenade deck. "Just in case you ever want to get someone out of your bedroom quickly," George explained. Thankfully, mine never got used. Mind you, my day cabin was nothing if not splendid and I could regularly entertain a dozen passengers for dinner or drinks in comfort, and often did. I remember on one occasion we had been joined by an Italian lady and her beautiful young daughter. At just 22, the girl was by far the youngest of the group and was particularly stunning. Lush red lips, a voluptuous figure and a mane of thick, dark hair – a true Italian princess. She soon had the officers who dined with us, and the stewards who attended on us, totally captivated. As we finished dinner, I was having such a lovely time with the group that I turned to her and asked, "I wonder if you would care to join me in my suite for coffee and a nightcap."

The girl blushed and gave a somewhat perplexing answer in her heavily accented English, "I would love to, but I am afraid I haven't taken any precautions".

It took a moment to realise what she meant, upon which I quickly reassured her, "That won't be a problem because I am sure your mother and the rest of our table will be joining me as well!"

One thing was certain, there was something in the sea air that affected women in strange ways – often completely robbing them of any inhibition. The length and destination of the cruise usually dictated the class and age of women that would be aboard. Longer cruises were the domain of the aged widow, spending her dearly departed's fortune with the mantra, "It's what he would have wanted" as they coyly flirted with the much younger officers. Shorter European cruises attracted a bevy of young beauties, and the crew certainly made the most of those occasions.

"Looks like there are a few ladies on board who could help you get into the Needles Club today?" I joked with one of the officers as we left Southampton. The Needles Club was something like the Mile High Club, only for cruise ships. On cruises out of Southampton, officers who wanted initiation into the club had to bed a passenger before the ship reached the Needles – the most southerly point of the Isle of Wight. The ship usually reached it in about an hour or so, meaning that only the most smooth-talking, fast-moving officers could gain entry to the club. Every officer was under oath to be truthful about his conquests to make the club, and perhaps it was the sexy, swaying motion of the ship that did it, but, surprisingly, it turned out to be not that hard to get into!

"I qualify for membership of the Needles Club," a panting, red-faced young engineer ran up to me on the bridge one day about three-quarters of an hour out of Southampton.

"Oh really," I joked. "Well, you know the rules. Point her out."

He was only too happy to accompany me to the public rooms to point out his conquest. "That one there. A beauty isn't she!" he gestured subtly.

"That one there?" I nodded my head in the good woman's direction.

He nodded and winked.

"Impossible!"

"What…! No way! It's true Commodore. I promise."

"Impossible. I know her … and her husband. There's no way."

"There WAS a way!" he insisted.

His paramour was one of Jean's closest friends, who was accompanying her husband on the ship at our invitation. Eventually, I was able to confirm the truth of the young engineer's claim, but it was many years before Jean would believe it.

"Commodore, I can't find my wife anywhere? I haven't seen her since we departed and I am very worried." A flustered husband approached me one day shortly after the ship had sailed from Las Palmas. There is so much to do onboard and so many different decks, shops and activities that it is not uncommon for partners to lose track of each other during the cruise. It was usually remedied by the purser putting out a call for the lady in question to contact reception. Several calls were sent out with no response, and I began to get a little worried myself.

"Have one of the stewardesses go in and check all of the ladies toilets on board," I instructed officers. "It's a little choppy today, perhaps she's taken ill in there." But the woman was still nowhere to be found.

"Hello, you haven't had any of our passengers contact you have you? We are missing a woman and I wondered if she might have been left behind." I radioed the agent at Las Palmas to ensure she wasn't stranded at our departure port.

"Commodore," the chief steward approached me, speaking in a whisper. "Have you checked the night steward's cabin? He ordered announcements to his cabin to be cut off during the day, so he could sleep."

Of course! The night steward had a well-deserved reputation with the ladies. We immediately dashed down to the crew quarters – just in time to see the missing woman furtively creep out of the night steward's cabin. She was totally ignorant of the fact that the entire ship had been frantically searching for her for more than an hour! Gossip spreads fast on board, no matter how hard you try to contain it, and where she was and just what she had been doing quickly became common knowledge. Her husband refused to speak to her for the rest of the cruise and she was followed around the decks by accusatory stares, pointing and giggling from the other passengers. I don't think she enjoyed the cruise much after that experience!

As commodore, I did my level best to stay out of trouble, but even I had some ladies make suggestions to me that I couldn't repeat here – if only so I don't embarrass my grandchildren! Even the most sophisticated women could be surprisingly lewd on occasion when surrounded by men in uniform. One day I was stopped by an elegant American woman in one of the public lounges.

"Mah husband was a naval officer, you know, Commodore," she drawled. "Ah was terribly sorry ah missed the official tour of the bridge, this mornin'".

"I'm on my way up there now, Madam, if you would like to accompany me," I offered, gallantly extending my arm. "I would be happy to give you a personal tour of the bridge."

"Why thank you very much," she took my arm.

"And this controls the ship's heading…" I showed her, noticing her apparent disinterest. She leaned in towards me.

"Ya know we could ahlways nip into your cabin, Commodore, to get friendly if you know what ah mean?"

I did know what she meant – and I wasn't happy about it in the least!

"Now Maam, I have an important meeting I have to attend," I curtly informed her. "Steward, will you please escort this lady back to the public areas."

I was shocked by her forwardness, but she was apparently shocked by my rejection. That evening I was approached by another American woman.

"Ah heard how you tried to force my friend into your cabin," she hissed. "Why you oughta be ashamed of yourself, Commodore. And I will have you know I intend to write to the chairman of Fourwinds Cruises to have you dismissed."

I did not tell her that the chairman of Fourwinds Cruises was me, but I was livid.

"I want to make two points," I replied sternly. "The first is that I would NEVER compromise my position on board by engaging in the lewd behaviour you have just suggested. The second is that you can tell your friend I wouldn't touch her with a barge pole."

She huffed and puffed but beat a hasty retreat.

THE GOLDEN YEARS

Cruises on *La Palma* had been such a success that Fourwinds soon expanded and our operations ushered in golden years for our parent company, Cotsworld Travel. John Batchlor and I began to reap some serious financial rewards in the 1980s as we added ever greater itineraries and more and more ships to our fleet. By this time, six months of my year were spent at sea, cruising the Mediterranean in the summer, the Norwegian Fjords in spring, and North Africa, Madeira and the Canary Islands in the winter. It was an idyllic lifestyle, although, strangely, I probably wasn't cut out to be a sailor. I was seasick more times than anyone I ever met and I never did conquer that nauseating feeling that accompanies the pitching of a ship in heavy swell. I became the world's greatest expert on seasickness! Even in the depths of winter, when we lurched through the Bay of Biscay, I insisted that all the ship's officers change into their whites as soon as Cape Finisterre was in sight. It gave the illusion of good weather, even while the ocean boiled on. As well as frequently sailing as commodore on *La Palma*, I also sailed on our charter ships – *Ocean Princess*, *Europa*, my old *Black Watch* (now renamed *Jupiter*) and several vessels we chartered on the Rhine. While some of the other big boys in the shipping industry were sailing half empty ships, ours were always full, for one simple reason: marketing. Reader offers remained our bread and butter and we sold many thousands of holidays a year thanks to our adverts in national and provincial newspapers and magazines like Woman's Own, TV Times and Farmer's Weekly.

'JOIN THE MAGNIFICENT *DAILY MIRROR* CRUISE TO THE GREEK ISLANDS' the headline screamed up from the Mirror. Bookings would roll in almost immediately and, true to my word, the newspaper's cut remained 10 per cent of all revenue generated. However, if a newspaper didn't produce any bookings, they didn't get paid for the advertisement. It was a guaranteed, cost-effective way to market. When I wasn't at sea, my whole family would help out with marketing the cruises. Jean, Terry, Michelle and I would all attend promotional evenings that were solely designed to convince prospective passengers to take a cruise. We would show a film of the ship and answer questions. I can't imagine many senior officers from today's cruise ships attending promotional events in their time off. Then again, not many of them pick up £100,000 in a single evening.

Cotsworld Travel also operated thousands of land-based holidays to other European destinations. My personal favourite was Austria and I took myself down there whenever possible to maximise our earning potential. Our tours to Leogang, not far from Salzburg, were so successful that on one occasion, when we managed to fill just about every hotel and guesthouse in town, I was given the freedom of the town. My limited shore time also included promotional trips to Holland, France, Germany and Italy to sell summer cruises from Venice to the Greek Islands through our European-wide network of agents. Of all the cruises, I most enjoyed those that had a high proportion of Italian passengers, because, from a crew perspective, they were the easiest to please. My least favourite passengers were the Scots, with the English and Australians not far behind them. Occasionally, every ship has problems of some sort that inconvenience the passengers. It is just a fact of life on board ship and the crew's job is to minimise the inconvenience as much as possible. Let's say, for example that a temporary generator problem means the kitchen can only serve cold food one lunchtime. The announcement would be made: 'We are sorry to inform you that due to a slight problem with a generator, which is being worked on, we will only be serving cold meat, seafood and salad for our buffet lunch today. We apologise for the inconvenience and would like to offer all of you free wine with today's buffet.'

The Italian passengers, far from being put out, would sit happily in the sun with a plateful of cheese, bread, tomatoes and luncheon meat that they washed down with free wine. In contrast, Scottish passengers, when facing the same 'crisis', would immediately form a queue at reception to ask what compensation they would receive. The English and Aussies will likely drink the free wine first, then ask what their compensation is! The other thing that made the Italians stand out as passengers was their almost innate sense of style. They positively gleamed on formal evenings and would be dancing, laughing and enjoying themselves while the Scots were arguing with the barman about whether a whiskey measure was a fourth or fifth of a gill. Along with the Scots and the English, German and French passengers were sometimes problematic too, although their main complaints were that there wasn't enough entertainment or food to suit their taste, which was probably true. Most of our group artists and musicians catered for all tastes, but the same could not always be said of our solo performers and comedians.

"Orright Guv'nor," Stan Boardman, our roguish Liverpudlian comedian, greeted me when I called him over a few hours before he was due to go on stage. He insisted on calling me 'Guv'nor' and also usually insisted on telling jokes that poked fun at some of our European passengers.

"No German or French jokes tonight, please Stan. We've a number of both nationalities on board and I don't want to upset them."

"Guv'nor, I wouldn't dream of it," Stan swore, looking me dead in the eye, solemnly.

"Excellent."

Later that evening, I invited some French and German passengers to join my table in the show lounge, just as Stan began his routine.

"Any Germans in the room? Any Germans? Come on, own up. I want all the Germans here tonight to put their hand up."

The German man at my table raised his hand hesitantly and a number of other hands around the room were also raised.

"Now put both hands up so you look more familiar!" Stan quipped.

I blushed with embarrassment as my German tablemate glared.

"I hear we've also got some French people on board tonight," he continued. "I've a question for you Froggies. Why are you the most miserable nation in Europe? And why would they want to build Disneyland right in the middle of the most miserable country in Europe? As soon as they built Disneyland the first thing you did was barricade all your ports so we couldn't bring our kids to see Mickey Mouse. Now, here's my question: Where were all the barricades when the Germans were coming in 1940? You didn't rush to set them up then, did you?"

"I'm so sorry. He gets a little carried away sometimes." I apologised to my po-faced dinner companions. The Germans were also often the reason for British complaints, largely due to their annoying habit of reserving sun loungers and deck chairs by the pool by leaving towels, books or other personal items on them for the entire cruise. Thankfully, it was a complaint that was easily remedied on the ships I sailed on. I would simply put through a call on the loudspeakers: "This is the commodore speaking from the bridge. In keeping with the ship's policy, I would like to inform all passengers that in fifteen minutes time I will instruct stewards to tour the open decks and remove all personal property from unoccupied seats. Any property can be claimed from reception this evening." I used to quite enjoy watching the selfish seat-reservers scramble to pick up the belongings that they had 'barred' seats with hours before they intended using them. On one occasion, thankfully not on one of my ships, I even encountered a man who had acquired an 'out of order' sign and hung it on a washing machine in the laundry for the duration of a cruise. It meant he could do his laundry at any time and be guaranteed a machine. I was disgusted by this act of selfishness, but it didn't come from a German – the man was British and left me despairing at the behaviour of some of my countrymen.

A lot of British people will tell you we are not a nation of complainers. I can tell you that is far from true. The British would begin queuing for lunch an hour before lunch was served and then complain about the wait. When we arrived in ports of call, they would rush to block the gangway and then whine that it took so long to get off because they couldn't all disembark at once. On one particular cruise, we had to call the emergency services just off shore from Ushant because an elderly passenger had suffered an aneurysm. While we were waiting for a Royal Navy helicopter to airlift the poor woman off, we lolled and rocked in heavy swell. The big Sea King arrived at about 1 am. It was a tense time on board as we battled the swell while attempting to align the ship with the helicopter at the right angle so a winchman could be lowered to lift the agonised woman off deck. I was in radio contact with the pilot when a ruddy-faced, rotund passenger stormed onto the bridge.

"I can't SLEEP," she yelled. "The air conditioning in my cabin is too noisy. Now it's woken me up and I can't get back to bed."

"Madam, it's not the air conditioning. It's the Sea King helicopter outside your cabin window, which is here to airlift a critically ill patient off the ship."

I waited for the woman's apology and look of embarrassment, but neither came. "Well for God's sake move the damn thing to the other side of the ship!" she demanded petulantly. I was gobsmacked. Unfortunately, the story had no happy ending. The sick passenger was safely transferred to the helicopter, only to die later in hospital. Sad as the story was, I have to say I was relieved the woman had not died on the ship. Few things are as upsetting for passengers and crew as a death on board.

MAN OVERBOARD!

Death on board comes quite frequently on cruise ships, probably due to the advanced age of some of the passengers. I would describe some of the deaths that occurred on board during my career as good deaths. If a 90-year-old expires halfway through dinner on the last night of a world cruise then that's a 'good death' in anyone's terms and I would certainly take it. But, of course, we had our fair share of terrible deaths too, particularly those that occurred by accident. Contrary to popular belief, a death at sea doesn't always result in a sea burial, and certainly not before the coroner has given permission. What happens to the body depends on whether the cruise is a line voyage or a short journey that returns to the original port of embarkation. On a long cruise, the body is usually taken ashore by the local undertaker at the next port of call and the poor relatives then arrange the complicated business of getting their beloved back home. If the ship is returning to its original port within a week or two, the body is kept on board, either in a special, refrigerated compartment, or in a coffin with its own cooling unit. While sea burials do take place, they are rare and it is more usual that someone's ashes would be scattered at sea after a cremation ashore.

By far the worst kind of death for staff onboard our cruise ships was 'man overboard'. We had to deal with that twice during my career. The first was a clear-cut case of suicide. The middle-aged male passenger had been travelling alone and was a dejected sort. He vanished, along with his luggage, into the North Atlantic in the middle of the night. He left behind nothing but a suicide note for his family, sadly explaining why he had decided to take his own life, a note for me apologising for any convenience he caused, and an envelope thoughtfully containing a tip for his steward. The second man overboard was far less straightforward.

"I've been by myself all day, why on earth wouldn't you think I was upset?" the elderly man admonished his much younger companion.

"Shhh, you're being foolish and embarrassing, and making a scene." The younger man was right about that. Few passengers in those days were openly homosexual and their very public row was causing titters among the other passengers. They retired, bickering, to their cabin and few thought any more about it, until the young man called at the purser's office the following day.

"I need you to put out a call for my partner. I haven't seen him since yesterday evening and I'm getting worried."

We put out the call, and then another, but all proved fruitless. We never saw that old man again. Did he jump or was he pushed? That was the question and it never received an answer. We couldn't tell and neither could the police, who were immediately brought on board. An open verdict was recorded at the inquest, which was conducted without a body having ever been found. As well as passengers who went missing, we also had a few who were unexpectedly 'found'. In those days, security was not considered of major importance aboard ship and stowaways could be a problem.

"All visitors ashore please. The ship is about to set sail," the loudspeaker would blare three times as we prepared to depart port. This was considered enough to ensure anyone who had not booked a cruise would disembark – of course, it wasn't! One stowaway was so determined that we had to kick him off the ship more than once! We were sailing the *Black Watch* from Las Palmas to Tilbury when an officer rushed up to me.

"We've just found a stowaway sleeping in a lifeboat," he told me. "What should we do with him?"

When we reached Tilbury we were turning around and heading back to Las Palma to do an identical cruise and there was no chance of the British police allowing him to leave the ship in a UK port.

"Lock him up for the time being. We'll keep an eye on him and hand him to the authorities once we get back to Las Palmas so they can deal with him there."

We made sure our unwelcome lodger got plenty of food and exercise and, in hindsight, we were probably too lenient on him for the week it took for us to arrive back in the Canaries. When we reached Las Palmas, we left our stowaway in the hands of our agent and sailed off again. Two evenings later,

141

another officer approached me "Guess what? Our mate's back."

"What do you mean?"

"Our stowaway. He's managed to get on board again. Must have enjoyed it too much last time," he grinned.

This time, we were a lot harder on him. We made sure he didn't enjoy his second trip back to the Canaries half as much and our agent promised to keep him strictly within his sight until we had sailed again. That cruise proved incident free, until we passed our sister ship the *Black Prince* on our way back to the Canaries.

"Hi Thor," I chatted with the captain of the *Black Prince* on the radio, as was customary when we encountered one of our own. "How is everything aboard today?"

"Well Terry," he sounded somewhat embarrassed. "I heard you recently had a persistent stowaway?"

"Yes we did, but we've managed to get rid of him this time, it seems."

"Yes, that is because he's now onboard the *Black Prince*," the captain told me matter of factly. I never did discover what happened to that stowaway but he managed to enjoy at least three of our cruises with few repercussions.

Our ships' security was rarely seriously breached in those days, however, and terrorism was hardly a concern, but there were a few occasions when we had a close call. Two of them occurred around Port Said, Egypt. On the first occasion, we had berthed at Port Said for two days during a cruise to Israel, Egypt and Turkey. Shortly after we departed, an Italian ship named the *Achille Lauro* moved onto the berth we had vacated. Suddenly the airwaves crackled with panic. The *Achille Lauro* had been hijacked by Palestinian terrorists, demanding Israel release fifty Palestinian prisoners. You may remember it [1985] because the terrorists cruelly killed 69-year-old American Jew Leon Klinghoffer, tossing the disabled man overboard in his wheelchair. The hijacking played out for two days before the terrorists surrendered. All I could think was that it so easily could have been us. Understandably, whenever we sailed into Port Said after that I was a little bit jittery and a few years later my nerves got the better of me. We were on an almost identical cruise of Israel, Egypt and Turkey aboard the *Ocean Princess*, and as we approached Egypt I got a call over the radio from the authorities at Port Said.

"Please be aware, we can confirm the presence of a group of known terrorists in the port area. We believe they may be targeting cruise ships."

I immediately contacted London.

"We've had an alarming security warning. Could you please tell me the names of all other cruise ships in the Port Said area?" I requested.

"You are currently the only cruise ship in the area," I was told.

I am simply not so brave that I was prepared to make my ship the sole target of terrorists! My announcement to the passengers had to be phrased carefully. I had to inform them that I was turning round and heading in the opposite direction because of a very real threat that the ship was to be the target of a terrorist attack, but I didn't want to throw them into a state of panic. Almost as importantly, I didn't want them all demanding their money back. This is what I said: "I have just received information from security forces in Port Said that the *Ocean Princess* is to be the target of a terrorist attack if we enter the port. If we are to be targeted by terrorists, they will no doubt know our itinerary. I hope you will agree with me when I tell you that I am turning the ship around and heading in the opposite direction. But I can promise you all a cruise that will be just as interesting and memorable." Realistically I had little idea where to head. After the announcement, I was straight back to the charts, desperately trying to figure out where we could sail to and still arrive at a decent time. "We have to come up with something," I urged the navigation team, "or we'll have everyone demanding a full refund! What about here?" I pointed to the little known port of Varna, in communist Bulgaria. "If we sail around the bottom of Turkey and into the Black Sea we should be able to make Varna in good time."

The problem was getting a cruise ship into a communist port at short notice. I contacted our office in London, the Bulgarian Embassy, and the Port Authorities in Varna with the same request. "This is the cruise vessel *Ocean Princess*. We need confirmation of a berth in the port of Varna and transit visas for our passengers."

Our London office said they would do what they could. We had no reply from either the Bulgarian embassy or the Port of Varna. Even as we approached the pilot station at 6 am two days later, I still hadn't received permission and wasn't sure what we would find when we got there, or even if they would let us in.

"Please wait at the pilot station for further instructions," the pilot told me. He was less than helpful and as we waited at the station, about a mile or so out from the port's entrance, I was worried about our prospects. We wallowed out there near the pilot station for more than two hours, and the passengers grew more and more restless. I was certain this port was going to be a disaster and I would have passengers queuing for refunds any minute. Eventually, the pilot boat approached and the pilot boarded the *Ocean Princess* with a huge smile on his face. I stood at his side as he gave precise instructions to the bridge team to guide the ship towards the entrance. As we pulled into the port, the reason for his grin became apparent. There, attired in Bulgarian national costume and lining the quay, were all of the children of the town. They were all smiling radiantly as they handed out posies of flowers to our disembarking lady passengers. The people of this tiny town had delayed our arrival to give them time to organise one of the most heart-warming welcomes I have ever experienced at any port around the world!

Our unexpected detour turned into a wonderful day. It was customary in Varna to hold group weddings and it turned out that we had arrived on a day when there were about a dozen weddings taking place. The village square rang with celebrations late into the night and we were all invited to spend the evening dancing, singing and celebrating with our new friends. I was delighted with Varna, but even more delighted when we had the chance to extend our thanks. Late the following afternoon, the town ice-cream man arrived. The hundreds of children who had given us such a spectacular welcome again formed a queue, this time each carrying a dilapidated square of cardboard. Ice-cream in Varna, it turned out, was a paltry affair. The vendor had an old-fashioned container strapped to the front of an old tricycle and in return for a coin, would splash a teaspoonful of sorry-looking ice-cream onto a cardboard square, which the delighted children would then lick off slowly. "We can do much better than this," I thought as I hurried back on board.

"How much ice-cream have we got?" I asked the provisions master.

"We've got a whole cold room full of it, of course."

"Great. I want it out here, on trestle tables on the wharf." I gathered the catering staff. "Set up the tables on the quay and go the whole hog – white tablecloths and a dozen of you guys from the galley in your best whites. I want every child to have a monster portion of ice-cream. Get the ship's photographer out there too."

The kids loved it. The passengers loved it. And the staff loved it. It was a wonderful opportunity for PR as the staff helped fill plastic dishes for the kids. I think it probably hastened the downfall of communism!

"Ladies and gentleman," the maître d' announced after dinner that evening. "I'd just like to inform you that WE HAVE NO MORE ICE-CREAM!"

The passengers cheered and clapped and not one of them asked for a refund. Varna had turned out to be one of the most memorable ports ever. Nowadays, Varna has progressed beyond recognition, with lovely new villas and golf courses. I must get back there when I can, because it strikes me as the perfect place to invest in a holiday home.

With all the talk of drunkenness and unruly passengers aboard cruise ships these days, I can say that my experience was very different and our passengers were generally charming and genteel. Only one of our security scares came at the hands of a passenger. Every Sunday we ran a regular church service and invited distinguished guests to read from the scriptures if they wished. At the time, we had Howard Bell, president of his branch of the Royal National Lifeboat Institute and a dear friend of mine, on board.

"Mr Bell has kindly offered to read from the scriptures for us today," I told the congregation as Howard stepped forward. As he did so, a passenger in his early forties dashed onto the stage. He brandished a paper bag in his right hand.

"I'VE GOT A GUN," he screamed. "And I'm taking over this ship." He spun around to look at me, rolling his eyes madly. That was to be his undoing because it meant he had to turn his back on our chief engineer. With lightning speed, the chief engineer tackled him and pinned him to the ground, restricting the movement of the would-be hijacker's right arm. The villain immediately started to sob and it did not take long for us to discover that the paper bag contained nothing more ominous than a book.

"Take him down to a secure cabin," I instructed. "And call the ship's doctor." When we and the ship's doctor cross-examined him we quickly realised he had some serious psychiatric issues. He had been travelling on the cruise with his mother, but we decided not to take any chances. Instead, they would both disembark at our next port of call, which happened to be Tenerife, where we would arrange for our agent to book them a flight back to London. We kept him securely locked away until we reached Tenerife, by which time he had quietened down considerably. Mental illness is a terrible affliction and I would like to be able to tell you that the man sought treatment and that this story, at least, had a happy ending. Unfortunately, it did not. The poor chap hanged himself within a few hours of disembarking.

AROUND THE EDGES

By the mid 1980s, cruising had become very much a family affair for us Hopleys. Michelle had grown up and married Martin, a man I am proud to call my son-in-law, although like all fathers-in-law I guess I was wary of him at first. I remember when I first met him, over dinner in a local pub, I rolled my eyes when I asked what he would like to drink and ended up having to order a strange concoction known as a snakebite, which consisted of a pint of beer mixed with what looked like a tequila sunrise. My first thought was, "Here we go, he couldn't just drink something normal!" Thankfully it didn't take me long to warm to him, snakebite or no snakebite. Together, Terry and Martin ran the hotel department aboard *La Palma*, overseeing more than 100 stewards with a budget of many millions for food and wine. They made a great team. Terry was still single, but was growing into a quite a playboy on board the cruises and enjoying his young adulthood.

Having so many of my family on board for so much of the year was often something of a distraction, but nevertheless one that I enjoyed. I was regularly accompanied by Jean, my dear mum and my other relatives. Michelle soon produced another tiny surprise for me – a little bundle of joy in the shape of my first granddaughter, Gemma. It was a wonder we had any room for passengers! While my siblings Jessie and Sam came on board only once (both were terribly seasick and vowed never to do it again, but did cruise with me later on the Rhine), Sheila and mum both enjoyed being on board. Mum, in fact, was hardly ever ashore and had become quite the party girl. The first time I invited her aboard *La Palma* she was accompanied by my Aunt Mary and my Uncle John. All were cockneys unused to the kind of opulence the ship offered and I was excited about spoiling them. To them, luxury was a pint of guinness and a cheese roll, so it wouldn't be hard to impress them, but I had still reserved the best suite on board for mum and a lovely two-bedded cabin next door for my aunt and uncle. Of course, I had the usual ship's duties and staff meetings to attend to before we left our home port, but dashed to mum's suite as soon as I could before we departed. I arrived in the suite to find mum sitting straight-backed and red-faced in the white leather sofa, with John and Mary propped up bolt upright in identical armchairs. As usual, the steward stood to attention when I entered.

"Ooh, you look lovely in your uniform," Aunt Mary cooed. "Turn around and let me have a look at the back. Don't he look smart, Jess?" Aunt Mary brushed at the back of my jacket and oohed and ahhed as she inspected the gold braid of my sleeves and cap at the back. The steward's eyes watered merrily and I could tell he could hardly believe what he was seeing and was dying to burst out laughing. To take some of the heat off me, I thought I would send the steward off to get some food for them all.

"Are you hungry, mum? Dinner's still a few hours off but I can get the steward to bring you a snack if you like?"

"How about a nice ham sandwich," mum suggested, but before I could turn to the steward to send him to the galley, she fished a foil-wrapped parcel out of her handbag and waved it gaily.

"Would you like one, darling," she asked the startled steward.

"Mum, we've got plenty of food on board the ship," I told her, by now rather embarrassed that my dear old mum was the first ever passenger to bring her own packed lunch.

"Oh yes, but it's lovely fresh ham, Terry. I only bought myself this afternoon!"

I had to escape the steward (who now had a visible twinkle in his eye), so I invited them up to the bridge to watch us sail away. (Mum's sandwiches at least offered the relief of portability!) The three of them watched in silence as the officers on the bridge barked out orders to let go the lines, and I stood next to the pilot as he conned the ship from its berth and out towards the open sea. But as the shoreline slipped behind us, it became too much for Aunt Mary.

"Oi, Terry, we're getting a bit far away from the edge," she worried, straining her eyes towards the distant land. "Turn the ship a bit closer to the coast."

"Don't worry, Aunt Mary, in another hour you won't be able to see any land at all," I informed her. "And then we won't see land again for another three days."

"Oh, don't be stupid, Terry. How are you going to find Madeira if you can't see where you're going?"

My poor auntie really thought we were going to go all the way around the edge to the Canaries! I have to admit though, that, as amusing as Aunt Mary's assumption was, it was not the silliest thing I ever heard from a passenger. Over the years, passengers frequently astounded me with their comments, such as: "I didn't realise there were two sittings for dinner; I don't think I can manage them both".

"Does the ship generate its own electricity?"

"Do all the crew sleep on board?"

"What do you do with the ice carvings after they melt?"

Or this, from an elderly lady whose husband had unfortunately died on the first night of the cruise: "Will he still qualify for 200 cigarettes and a bottle of whiskey when we go through customs?"

On some occasions, I found it hard to answer seriously. When asked. "Why is the ship zig-zagging?" I once naughtily answered, "Because we are in a minefield."

Despite my aunt's shock at our navigation techniques, my family had a lovely time. They quickly decided not to use the two-bedded cabin in favour of Mary sharing the king-size bed with my mum and poor Uncle John sleeping on the sofa with a duvet. I'll never forget visiting that luxury suite the first morning at sea to find the white marble sideboard decorated with three glasses of Steradent, each complete with bobbing false teeth. After several days of watching mum and my aunt and uncle living it up on board, we sat down to breakfast one morning only to find mum complaining that most of the food was too hard for her to chew.

"My teeth are killing me today," she winced as she took a sip of tea. Just as I was about to suggest a visit to the ship's hospital, I noticed that Uncle John's smile was slightly askew. Sure enough, they had got their teeth mixed up!

""Terry, that nasty machine beat me again. Why don't you open it up for me," mum pointed to one of the one-armed bandit machines in the ship's casino. She loved playing the machines and had figured out an infallible system, which worked only because she was the commodore's mum. Every morning she would have me change £20 in ten pence pieces for her day's gambling. If she lost, she would persuade me to get the machine opened up and give her the money back. If she won, she was surprisingly quiet and said nothing. The company who had the concession had little option but to go along with it. After mum's first cruise, it was almost impossible to get her off the ship, but she was my mum, so even when the cruise was packed I almost invariably managed to set her up in an expensive suite on board.

"I'm sorry, Mum, but the ship is full – completely full," I apologised on one of the rare occasions when I couldn't find a cabin. "You'll just have to go home for a couple of weeks and then we'll get you back on next time. I promise."

"I don't mind, I'll share with someone else," she volunteered.

"Mum, I just don't think that passengers who've spent thousands of pounds on a cruise are going to be happy to find they have to share their cabin with the commodore's mum."

"Well, Terry, that's ok. I'll just have to sleep with you in your bed."

I could only imagine how great that would be for my reputation! But she insisted on being aboard so I eventually converted a hospital cabin into a temporary suite for her and off she went again back to the casino. Luckily, my party-loving mum was always popular with the staff and the passengers, so no one seemed to mind that she was such a regular passenger.

Having my son on board once caused me embarrassment of a different kind – when the staff captain approached me one day to tell me that Terry was breaking the ship's rules for officers by fraternising with crew members. The crew member in question happened to be our new beauty therapist. When I had set up the onboard salon, I was aided by our super-efficient departmental coordinator, Sarah Lloyd – a girl so pragmatic and organised that her nickname was 'the commodore in waiting'. The very first beauty therapist Sarah hired was vivacious and pretty eighteen-year-old Tracy Keener. Very pretty, my son Terry obviously thought! I mulled over the problem for a few hours then called Terry to my cabin.

"Just what do you think you're playing at," I warned him off. "You know its against policy for officers to invite crew members to their cabins. There can't be one rule for you and one rule for everyone else, so you'll just have to call it off."

Terry was having none of it.

"Too late for that, Dad. I think I'm in love with her," he admitted. Terry's bachelor days were drawing to an end.

"What should I do?" I asked Jean, "Should I get her to leave the ship. I can't have the others thinking Terry's getting special treatment.'

"Why don't you talk to her first," Jean suggested. "After all, you haven't even met her."

I rang down to Sarah. "Can you please send Tracy Keener up to my cabin. I need a manicure and I've heard she's very good." I thought that would give me a chance to have a chat with her and find out whether she thought her relationship with Terry was that serious or whether it was just a summer fling.

Tracy arrived at my cabin about half an hour later. Terry was right, I thought, she was devastatingly beautiful, albeit a little shyer than I predicted. She trembled as she picked up the nail scissors. Just as she began to snip I asked: "So Tracy, I've heard that you are very friendly with my son Te….RRY! Argghgh!"

My sentence was swallowed by a loud yelp of pain as a nervous Tracy proceeded to slice not only my nail but also the tip off my finger.

"Oh, I'm so sorry, Commodore," she squealed as blood dripped on the carpet. My plans for a little chat were temporarily put on hold, but we have had plenty of time to chat since. Although Terry and Tracy are no longer together, Tracy is the mother of my four gorgeous granddaughters: Suzannah, Georgina, Gabriella and Amelia. Their marriage lasted 20, sometimes tempestuous, years before they made a mutual decision that divorce was the best option. Now Terry has a beautiful new partner, Vanessa, and between them they have seven very happy children.

Of course, I wasn't the only staff member to have family on board *La Palma*. Few ship owners spent as much time on board their vessels as George Louris; his family members were also frequent passengers.

"Commodore!" George greeted me one day on the bridge with his customary noisy kiss on each cheek. "Are all of our passengers on board?"

We were about to set sail from Venice with a new contingent of passengers and our departure time was set at 3 pm. I glanced at my watch, which read 2.40 pm. Passengers were always made aware of the sailing time and it was their responsibility to be back on board at least 30 minutes before departure. It can be very expensive to keep a ship in port beyond its scheduled departure time, so any passengers who weren't on board when the gangway was lifted were left behind. It was then their responsibility to find their way to the next port to continue the cruise. Usually, their excuse was that they were confused by the 24-hour clock, mistaking 1800 hours for 8 pm instead of 6 pm but we knew that if we gave them leeway with the departure time, people would take liberties.

"Yes George, they're all on. The pilot is on the bridge and the tugs are standing by. We are all ready for a three o'clock departure from the berth."

"Ah Commodore, I wonder if, for me – for George – you can make a special favour today? As a special favour, perhaps today we sail a little bit early?"

"I'll ask the pilot for you, George, but the tugs are in position so it should be possible," I told him, wondering why he was in such a hurry. The pilot assured me it wasn't a problem, so the remaining gangway was removed, I made a brief announcement to the passengers and we set off bound for the Adriatic, the Corinth Canal and Athens.

"Why were you so desperate to leave early today anyway, George?" I asked him later on when we were safely up to cruising speed. A cheeky, delighted grin spread over his face.

"My mother-in-law was still shopping in Venice. I told her, Terry, she must be back in plenty of time. I told her, so I want to teach her a lesson."

Sure enough, his annoyed mother-in-law had to fly from Venice to Athens to rejoin the cruise. She was never late back on board again.

OUT OF THE BLUE

"Happy eightieth birthday, Mum!" I smiled, kissing her cheek as I handed her the present I had bought for the occasion – a lap keyboard so she could play tunes without having to get up from her favourite armchair. Mum always had a musical talent and even played the drums for a band down at the local pub in her elderly years, but, at eighty, arthritis was getting the better of her. She was clearly pleased with the gift and with the large party we had thrown for her. Most of her grandchildren and great grandchildren attended, along with a host of friends. I wouldn't have missed it for the world. In fact, I had been on a Greek Islands cruise on *La Palma* but had flown home just for the event. It was only an overnight trip. The next day I was to fly back to Dubrovnik to rejoin the ship. As the driver took me back to Heathrow the next morning, I gave mum a call to say goodbye. I didn't realise it would be our last.

"Terry, listen to this," mum giggled as she played me a tune on the keyboard. She was full of fun and laughter, chatting to me about the party and my gift. It was only when I arrived back on the ship's gangway in Dubrovnik that I found something was wrong. The staff captain was waiting, glum-faced, at the bottom of the gangway.

"What is it?" I asked immediately, sensing bad news.

"Terry, I'm afraid it's your mother. She's passed away."

I was sure he was mistaken. After all, she had just turned eighty and I had only spoken to her a few hours ago, but it was true. At the time, a neighbour had popped around to take mum's bet for the afternoon's racing down to the bookmaker for her. As he was waiting for mum to write out her bet, she suddenly said: "I think I might need a drop of brandy first. I'm not feeling too well all of a sudden."

Before he could reach the drinks cabinet she was gone. As quickly as that mum's life was over. I turned around immediately for a flight back to England. "Whatever's going to become of us, now?" I thought.

Mum was a beautiful lady, a central part of our family and I have never loved anyone more than I did her. She is still sadly missed by her children, grandchildren and great grandchildren, and her funeral was one of the saddest days I have ever experienced. Having said that, I am thankful for small mercies, knowing that my mother went quickly, without the pain or suffering my dad endured. The older you get in life, the more death lurks in the shadows before coming out of the blue one day to steal away a friend or family member. But when you lose someone close to you, you want it to be a good death, the kind that comes suddenly and as painlessly as possible. Sadly, not all of my family members were to find such a peaceful passing from this life. My nephew Danny Boy died in a car crash at the tender age of twenty and his death sent my sister Sheila into a downward spiral. She died a year later of breast cancer, and, I believe, a broken heart. As much as I was able to bring some small joy to Sheila's life by taking her cruising, she often proved to be her own worst enemy. Her Irish husband was a drunkard and when they parted after twenty years, she became involved with another unsuitable man. He was a keen trap shooter and on the few occasions he came on board the ship he would be on the ship's stern every day, where trap shooting took place. Unfortunately, when he got home, he kept up the work with the shotgun and got himself ten years for armed robbery just before Sheila fell ill. My flirtatious, fun-loving sister certainly deserved more in life, but life doesn't always provide. Much more recently, another funeral added to the pain when Sam and I attended the funeral of our uncle. Uncle Terry died suddenly just before his 84th birthday. Although the deterioration in his health had been gradual, his body had been devastated by cancer nearly twenty years before. In his sixties, he had even had half his stomach removed and his weight plummeted to seven stones, but his fighting spirit refused to give in. He was still playing golf competitively and driving a car well into his eighties, and still occasionally threatened to flatten any troublemaker who got in his way.

As Uncle Terry still lived in Dagenham, we stayed with Jean's mum for a few days before the funeral.

"Typical!" I chastised myself the day before, realising that I'd forgotten my dark suit and tie. I dashed down to Marks and Spencer and bought a dark blue suit, a white shirt and black tie. My brother Sam and his wife Joyce drove me to the crematorium. It was a hot day, so I threw my suit jacket on the back seat until we arrived. As I watched the coffin disappear through the curtains and the clenched jaws and tears of my cousins, Kevin, Barry, Alan and Maureen – now all senior citizens like Sam and I, I couldn't help thinking of Uncle Terry in his sailor's uniform, with a superb body of muscle rippling beneath it and a neck like a bull. I guess it all comes to this in the end, but Uncle Terry was always ready to take on the world and, right to the end, he did. Afterwards, a buffet lunch was served and as Sam and I consoled relatives and friends, my brother suddenly realised that his jacket didn't match his trousers. He looked over at me, to realise that mine didn't match either. We had gone right through the funeral each wearing the other's jacket and neither of us had noticed! As he whispered it to me, the thought made me smile. If Uncle Terry was looking down on us that day, he would surely have had a few choice words to say.

BUSINESS, AS USUAL

As our golden years drew on, Fourwinds Cruises and our land-based division, Cotsworld Travel, continued to expand. Along with the ocean-going cruises, we were also taking passengers down the Rhine, which was a very different affair to operating a big liner. To begin with, on the Rhine we were definitely on a boat, rather than a ship. The difference between the two has been the topic of many arguments. Some used to say that ships are made of steel and boats of wood or fibreglass, but that is not strictly the case. A better distinction is that ships carry boats! The fact that ships are more substantial counted little on the Rhine. Our boats on those cruises were little more than 45 metres (147 feet) long – a fraction of the size of a cruise liner. I enjoyed being at the controls of these versatile vessels, handling the novel signalling system that indicates to other river traffic on which side you intend to pass. (The old rule of passing port to port does not apply on the Rhine.) As far as cruising time goes, the Rhine cruises were the opposite of sea cruises. On the Rhine, we would cruise all day and tie up at night. On ocean cruise liners, we usually sailed by night and tied up by day. Both the Rhine and Moselle have some beautiful stop-off points, but although our passengers loved the cruises on the boats they were never really as profitable. Making a profit, of course, became even more important as time went by because John and I were starting to talk about scaling back our ambitions and taking early retirement to enjoy our newfound wealth. By that stage, I was approaching my 50th birthday. Although John was ten years younger than me, we both felt it was time to look for ways to cash in.

"When we wind this up, I think I'd like to live in South Africa," John told me, "and do nothing but play golf."

Ironically, when the time came to sell Fourwinds Cruises, it was I who moved abroad, and even owned a golf course at one stage, while John attempted to carry on in the travel industry.

Earlier that same year, before John and I had discussed selling the company, we had purchased a lovely big house in Hucclecote, Gloucester, which we planned to convert into offices. Unfortunately, we didn't receive planning permission, so we were left with a big house and nothing to do with it.

"It's such a lovely old house, it is a shame to leave it empty," Michelle approached me one day. She was rarely on the ship by that time, having a young family to take care of, while her husband Martin spent several months of the year at sea.

"Dad, what about letting me convert it into a day nursery?" Michelle was a fantastic mother and day care was always going to be a necessity for parents, so I thought it was a rather entrepreneurial move from Michelle – not that I was surprised, because both of my children have inherited my business acumen. John wasn't really interested in moving into the nursery business, so I bought out his share of the house and gave it to Michelle. Michelle found great success with her Treetops Day Nursery and soon started up an even bigger school in Cheltenham as well. She now has more than 450 babies and toddlers under her care. However, despite her success, I sometimes think I made a mistake. You see, Michelle's highly regarded, professionally run nurseries prevent her family from joining the rest of the Hopley clan in Australia, and I miss my daughter and her family terribly when I am there.

Soon after, it was Terry's turn to demonstrate his creative business spirit. Terry and Tracy had been living in our house in Madeira, but reducing my cruise schedule and preparing to sell the business also meant, for me, tightening up some of my personal assets. I had immediately fallen in love with Madeira on my first cruise there. Initially, the friendliness of the locals drew me, and I was so impressed I even obtained Portuguese citizenship. As part of my new Madeiran lifestyle, I had shipped a beautiful new cabin cruiser to Madeira, along with a brand-new Ford Escort Cabriolet, prepared for me Cosworth-style by 'my' Ford Motor Company. When I imported them, my smiling friends in customs waved me through without paperwork; however, over the years, the easy-going nature of the local officials changed. As the years passed, Madeira became increasingly commercial, until it wasn't too different from Majorca or Tenerife. The change was gradual and as Madeira was one of the focal points of the cruises, Terry and Tracy spent much of the year there, organising incoming flights and looking after our passengers. We knew all the local haunts, so a regular feature of the ship's scheduled stop in Madeira was a trip to Miradorou, a lovely little restaurant in the mountains. Terry, Tracy, Jean and myself had discovered it one day and noticed that, although it could seat about 200 diners, it never contained more than about five. It was a great shame because although it had only one dish, that one dish was, without question, the most delicious barbecue piri-piri chicken you ever tasted. It was presented on a miniature barbecue in the centre of the table, and served with salad and fried maize. Even better, it was all you could eat, so whenever it ran low it was quickly replenished. The meal was washed down with limitless jugs of red wine. Afterwards, the owner would invite diners to his private cellar to drink Madeira from oak barrels, some of which were labelled 1936 or earlier. Everyone who stood in that cobweb-filled cellar agreed it tasted like nectar. (Much later, we found out he topped up the barrels from bottles each evening!) However, by far the best thing about dining at Miradorou was that it cost just £3. We weren't slow to see the potential. Soon, an excursion to this unique restaurant became a regular feature of the ship's itinerary in Madeira, and our passengers thought it was excellent value at £15 a head! We took hundreds of passengers up there each week and made a healthy profit.

The successful dinners at Miradorou soon led to another money spinner. When passengers from the ship visited Miradorou for the evening, it left numerous empty seats in the dining room. To compensate, we offered holiday-makers staying in local hotels dinner aboard a cruise ship. First, we had to deal with the small matter of customs and immigration, but that wasn't a problem in Madeira in those early days. On every call we made to the island, it was polite to invite the customs officers (together with their wives, kids and sometimes nan and grandad too) on board for lunch. If they wanted that privilege to continue, they co-operated and generally they did, until the whole arrangement was wrecked by a new head of customs, who cost me a fortune.

"What's taken you two so long," I called out, when I heard Terry and Tracy arrive back at our house in Sãn Gonçalo. A white-faced Terry entered the room.

"We've been down at the police station all afternoon. They stopped us in the car and demanded we produce the customs paperwork on the spot. Of course, we couldn't! They've impounded the car."

The next morning I immediately took a cab to the customs office in the harbour. I was convinced that once they realised it was my car it would be released. As I stepped out of the taxi, I noticed another familiar sight was missing from the harbour – my boat! Sure enough, that had been impounded too. All my pleadings at the customs office fell on deaf ears.

"You don't have the proper paperwork. No boat. No car." The new custom's official was adamant. The stalemate lasted for several months, during which time my protests were met with nonchalant shrugs from my former friends in customs. No more free lunches for them. Then, through sheer luck, a senior minister and his wife booked a cruise on *La Palma*.

"Commodore, thank you for looking after us so well," he pulled me aside on their last evening on board. "If there is ever anything I can do to repay you, please let me know."

"Actually…" I said, before launching into the sad story of my impounded car and boat. His reaction was immediate.

"Dad," Terry rang me excitedly the next day, "the car's back, complete with all the correct paperwork stamped and signed Madeiran style!"

"What about the boat?" I asked. But it was not to be. I have not seen it from that day to this. For all I know it is still bobbing around in the customs pound. After a couple of years, I simply gave up the fight. Given the trouble they had given me with the car, I quickly put it in the hold of the ship and brought it back to England. It was stolen within a week! So I never saw that again either. That incident demonstrated to me that the whole ethos of the island of Madeira had changed, and as I was starting to wrap up my cruising career, I decided to sell the house in Sãn Gonçalo. I put through a call to my friend Denis Pestana, who had helped me build it, and asked him to dispose of it on my behalf.

"Terry, you spend so much time on the ship, perhaps, in order to make a quick sale, it would be better if I had power of attorney," Denis suggested. Denis was a trusted friend and I had absolutely no hesitation in doing so. In fact, by the time I had turned the ship around and returned to Plymouth, Denis called to say he had sold it at a nice healthy profit to a South African purchaser. There was just one problem – the South African had already moved in! Unfortunately, Denis had sold it with all my possessions still inside.

We never got a thing back – no clothes, jewellery, crockery, bed linen or even photographs. They all went to the new owner, who wasn't prepared to listen to my pleas that I wanted them all returned.

The sale of the house in Madeira and my increasing desire to see Fourwinds become a public company had the potential to leave my son Terry out of a job, but he soon found something else to keep him occupied. Back in the Cotswolds, Bentham Country Club in Gloucester had gone into receivership and was going cheap. It consisted of a main building containing a restaurant, bar and function rooms plus two gigantic domes where tennis, bowling and other recreational sports were offered, but it was bleeding money. Our original plan was to turn part of it into a hotel and the rest into comfortable new offices for Cotsworld Travel and Fourwinds, but we were again unable to obtain planning permission to do so. After Terry had worked desperately for six months to turn it around, with little financial improvement, he cornered me one day with an idea.

"Dad this place can't work with bowls and tennis," he told me. "Five-a-side football is where the money is."

I backed Terry in running with his idea, and I'm very glad I did. The country club now runs extremely successful indoor five-a-side football, netball, tennis and hockey leagues. Terry's idea turned it around almost immediately.

I put a call through to my old friend Geoff Hurst, knowing that his involvement would guarantee publicity. "Geoff, how would you feel about opening our new country club in Gloucestershire, which is becoming a five-a-side indoor football venue?" Once again, it helped to have friends in high places. We alerted all the media that Geoff Hurst would be opening the club, and the phones soon rang hot with reporters telling us they would only be interested if Geoff Hurst was going to play.

"How long have we been mates?" I pleaded with Geoff, who had not pulled on a pair of boots for years. "Please, do me one more big favour. I need you to get your kit on and play," I begged. Thankfully, Geoff agreed, and, mirroring his world-cup winning effort, even scored another hat trick. Bentham Country Club now boasts the largest five-a-side soccer league in Europe and has a membership of more than 3000. Terry can be justifiably proud of his efforts, but life for him was soon to change too, and the club is now leased to our old friend Tony Markham, who has managed to make it even more successful.

While all this was going on, John and I were also making negotiations for one of the biggest business deals of our lives – the sale of Fourwinds Cruises and Cotsworld Travel.

NOBODY KICKS ME TWICE

I had always known leaving *La Palma* would be difficult, and that the day I stepped down the gangway for the last time would be a sad one, but a strange incident made leaving that grand old girl much easier. George had been unwell for some time and had begun to lose interest in the ship. There is an old saying that 'A Greek will always let you down,' but I had a long and loyal friendship with George and never thought the saying would apply to us. As it happens, it did, but it was an act of extreme loyalty on George's part that let me down and went a long way towards ending our association. One day, on my routine inspection of the ship, I popped into one of the small lounges in the early evening to find it silent. Knowing we had employed a Scots guitarist and his chanteuse daughter to liven up the lounge, I immediately called Frank Connor, our cruise director.

"Frank this place is like a morgue. Where are the two musicians?"

"It's that bl–dy Scots guitarist," Frank confessed. "He's refusing to play. Reckons there's a problem with his shower and he won't go on stage because of it. He's been holding us to ransom for a few nights now."

"Get one of the plumbers to sort out his shower, but tell him if he isn't in here playing tomorrow night he and his daughter are off the ship. We've all got a job to do here and cabin problems don't come into it."

The next evening, I returned to the lounge. It was still silent, and our musician was nowhere to be seen. It was an Adriatic and Greek Island Cruise and we were on our approach to Corfu at the time before sailing on to Venice.

"When we get to Venice, disembark them both," I gave the order. "And at the same time get another duo to fly out to Venice to replace them."

Later in the day I was approached by the surly Scots musician himself.

"Eff you, I'm fed up with the whole thing," he spat scornfully. "I'm not travelling one more effing day on this ship. I'm getting off tomorrow."

"That's the best news I've heard all day," I responded. "I only suggested you disembark in Venice to make it easier for you to transport your equipment back to Britain. But if you want to get off on a Greek island, feel free."

He stormed off, still swearing loudly.

The following day, I'd gone ashore at lunchtime to dine with some passengers. As I returned and made my way towards the gangway, who should I meet but the irate guitarist. He was exiting the ship at an extremely hurried pace (we later discovered he had sabotaged our entertainment equipment and microphones by cutting the cords). As he passed me, sneering, he flew at me and kicked me quite hard in the thigh. It was more embarrassing then painful, but it did leave a bruise and I was quite shocked that he would do such a thing in front of passengers. The skirmish was over in seconds as two burly sailors grabbed him by the throat and marched him out of sight. As we sailed out of Corfu that evening our Scots friend was back on the quay, and this time, in front of hundreds of passengers who were watching our sail-away, he dropped his pants and bent over to moon me.

"Good riddance to him," was my final thought on the matter until Manolis approached me some hours later.

"Commodore, Mr Louris wants you to spare him a moment before you go to dinner," he informed me. I made my way to George's cabin.

"Mwa…mwah," George greeted me with his customary effusive kiss on each cheek. "Commodore, I have heard this terrible, terrible news only just now!" he told me, in his usual melodramatic style. He was in such a state that I wondered what he was talking about and began steeling myself for a disaster.

"What news is that?" I asked.

George tapped his ear theatrically. "I have heard…this man today, he kicked you in front of the passengers."

"Yes," I admitted. "He has left me with a big bruise on my leg. But not to worry, he's gone now. He was a guitarist who was refusing to play so we kicked him off the ship, and he just happened to kick me back," I joked.

"No, no, no, no," George whistled through his teeth. "I have taken," he rubbed his hands together slowly then cracked the knuckles of his right hand ominously, "the necessary steps. It is over, Commodore. It is finished.

Katalaves? (You understand?) He will be run over tonight in Corfu."

For a split second I thought he was kidding, but I could see from the expression on his face he was deadly serious, and I was having none of it.

"No, George! It doesn't mean anything to me. In fact, I've forgotten all about it. It's not worth it!" I pleaded. George shook his head and frowned. I could see he was disappointed by what he perceived to be my weakness, but I had never seen him so callous before, and over such a little thing. His manner both scared and disturbed me.

"No, no, no," George repeated. "It means nothing to you because you are a stupid Englishman. But it means something to ME! If he kicks you – he kicks me. You are my commodore. There is no difference. No man will ever, EVER, kick me twice. He kicks me once – he's dead. It is finished!" he flicked his right hand dismissively. I knew there was no point in arguing with him; he was determined that our Scots guitarist be punished for this grave insult. I spent more than 15 years with the uneasy feeling that I had been directly responsible for the disappearance of a Scotsman in Corfu. The incident made me even more certain that selling the business and leaving was the right thing to do. Our friendship cooled after that incident, and George suddenly took off for the United States to treat the diabetes that was beginning to take a heavy toll on his body. I was never to cruise with him again.

SET FOR LIFE

After the unhappy episode with George, I decided to take some leave and flew back to Gloucester for increasingly serious negotiations with Cannon Street Investments. Both John and I liked what we heard and so, in 1990, we signed Fourwinds Cruises and Cotsworld Travel over to them in a deal that would make us both millionaires many times over. There was only one snag: because Cannon Street Investments was new to the cruise industry, we had to sign a service agreement that would tie us to the company for five years. As I was at sea during most of the contractual negotiations, and during the time of due diligence, it was decided that the contracts would be signed and exchanged on board *La Palma*. The team of solicitors and accountants came on board at Venice. Not surprisingly, they seemed to be able to find a good many issues with the contract, which kept them on board for at least a fortnight. I did notice that they appeared to have far more time for enjoying the varied pleasures of the cruise than for working through the intricacies of the contract. However, this may have worked in my favour because, as a "get out of jail free card", I had it written into my contract that, as commodore, no one could override any decision I made. To my advantage, they assumed this meant on board ship, but, in fact, the contract did not stipulate that, which, in effect, gave me the freedom to do anything I wanted. When they signed, shook my hand and announced I was now a very wealthy man, I was determined to give them their money's worth and keep the company moving forward for at least the next five years.

My first cruise after John and I sold the company was aboard an elegant little ship called *Danae*. We were to sail via the Canary Islands, Barbados, Panama Canal, the beautiful Tahitian Islands, Bora Bora and Raratonga to

New Zealand and then on to Australia. After all the wonderful places we visited on the way, Australia, I thought, was going to have to be pretty nice to impress me. But impress me it did. It was a cruise that would change my life, because Australia impressed me enough so that I now call the land down under my second home for six months of each year. Brisbane is a beautiful city, but it's not the most glamorous or well-known of Australia's state capitals. At the time of our visit, the Queensland government was trying to remedy that with an ambitious plan to build a new cruise-ship terminal in the hope of lifting Brisbane's profile by convincing a ship to operate permanently out of the city. The state government, through the Queensland Travel and Tourist Corporation, invited Jean and I back on a six-week visit to help them with their plans.

"Sure, I'd be glad to help," I offered, "But coming from Gloucestershire, we quite like to be out in the country, so if you could put us up somewhere out of the city, where we could truly enjoy the perfect weather, swim or go for a walk in the countryside, that would be much appreciated."

The Queensland government didn't disappoint. They booked a suite at the Hyatt Hotel in Sanctuary Cove. When I woke up that first morning and opened the shutters to be met with the warm Australian sun, I just knew that I would be spending a good part of my retirement right there. I didn't realise it at the time, but it would also introduce me to that time-consuming, forever-frustrating game – golf. I ended up spending six months in Australia, even flying the financial director of the company, Ian McClearie, out to investigate the possibility of basing a ship in Brisbane. However, in true bureaucratic manner, the government officials and ministers were moving at a far slower pace than I was prepared for and Sanctuary Cove's balmy luxury was making me increasingly restless for retirement. I was also becoming increasingly disillusioned with Cannon Street Investments.

Before we sold the company, the visionary chairman of Cannon Street Investments had become a firm friend and I had a lot of faith in him. Unfortunately, the other board members did not, because after we sold he was quickly removed in a boardroom coup and a young city whizz kid was installed in his place. His 'replacement' knew little about cruising and it was an understatement to say we didn't see eye to eye. When I returned to the UK, the proverbial hit the fan and I was summoned to the chairman's city office.

"Ah, Commodore," he greeted me, without wasting any time on pleasantries, "I have brought you here today to ask you just what the bloody hell you've been playing at."

"What a coincidence," I responded, sarcastically, as I sat down. "You see, I've come here today to ask what the bloody hell you've been playing at. When I left we were making millions and now it seems we're losing millions. My suggestion is that you either let me run Fourwinds Cruises the way it should be run and allow me to go back to making major decisions, as stipulated in my contract, or you take responsibility for this mess... in which case, I'll be on my way."

The next week, I was on my way. The company struggled on, trying to run ships without my help. Those city accountants quickly discovered that there was a lot more to running a successful cruise ship than adding up columns of figures. They made many grave errors that lowered their profit margins, such as installing an external catering contractor who charged around twelve pounds a day per passenger. With Fourwinds, we had an extremely high standard of catering because we ran it ourselves, at a cost of just seven pounds per head per day. I guess we were clever in that catering costs for wine were also reduced by a nice personal touch – buying my own vineyard. John and I became major shareholders in the 200-acre winery in the Cotswolds and our well-regarded Three Choirs wine won many prizes and quickly became the best-selling wine on board, enhanced by its description on the wine list – 'From the Commodore's personal vineyard'. I remained chairman of the Three Choirs Vineyard Ltd for several years and sometimes wish I still owned that boutique winery.

My partner, John, also initially worked for Cannon Street Investments, but in an office capacity rather than on the ships. Like me, he was soon fed up with the new owners. The chairman quickly paid him off and released him from the part of his contract that forbade him being involved with any other cruise-ship company, upon which he had a go at running another cruise company, Festive. Unfortunately, Festive never really returned the sort of profits he and I had enjoyed with Fourwinds during our halcyon days, and the company eventually crumbled. Our relationship has never been quite the same since, which is a great pity because he and I were as close as brothers during our golden years. Out of the ashes of Festive arose one of our former employees, Richard Ford. He took over the reins and formed a new company known as Travelscope. It grew to be the biggest in the business, which brought Richard many accolades. However, I still wish I had had the chance to show him how to make real profits for himself from cruising, rather than making ship owners richer than they ought to be. Eventually Travelscope also went into liquidation, despite operating three ships, which should have made them a fortune.

IN EXILE

"What is it about Australia that made you choose it as a second home?" is the question I am invariably asked when people realise I have travelled the world over many times. The Gold Coast is blessed with many great benefits (even aside from the more than 300 sunny days a year) although it took some time to convince my family of that. While I was on the ship, I was considered a non-resident of the UK because I took care not to spend more than 90 days at a time in Great Britain. This afforded me considerable tax advantages. When Fourwinds became a public company, I would have had to pay millions in tax had I chosen to reside in the UK. By my reckoning, I could hand half of my newfound wealth to the taxman or I could set up my children for life and take care of the education of my seven grandchildren. It was no contest! However, there are two things you cannot avoid, 'death and taxes' according to the old saying, so if I have to choose one of them for now, I'll take taxes! Despite the efforts of my accountants I still manage to pay an awful lot of tax. It seems I get a double whammy for each year, with one tax bill from the UK and another from the Australian Taxation Office, not that I dare complain. To achieve my exile as comfortably as possible, after my first stay in Sanctuary Cove I purchased three luxurious houses within the gated resort and convinced Jean, her elderly mum, Terry and Tracy, and Michelle and Martin to join us in Australia. It was no small feat, as it tore Michelle and Martin away from Treetops for a while and they had to sell their house to come. Once we got the issue of houses and schools sorted, I was sure everything would be perfect and I was delighted to have my entire family with me…that is, until the bickering began. Jean has never found it easy to move, and her mum had spent all of her life in Essex. Soon, we were all miserable as our wonderful new lifestyle began causing rows and arguments. Within months, they all flew home to England, leaving me alone in our big, empty new house. The word exile had never been more apt – I spent more than a few lonely months on my own. Since then, Jean and I have reached a compromise. We spend half the year in Australia and the rest split between England and the French Riviera, where I bought another luxury home. Terry and Tracy, at least, also eventually had a change of heart. After a few exploratory visits to Australia, they decided to seek permanent residence and moved to Sanctuary Cove in 2004 with their four daughters. Michelle and Martin and their family visit Australia often, but their hearts are firmly rooted in the UK where they own a magnificent home in Gotherington, in the heart of the Cotswolds. Geoff and Judith Hurst were harder to convince, but after a few visits, Australia became almost like a second home to them too, and they spend a couple of months here most years.

The start of my retirement was far from relaxing, however, because it was not long before I got myself involved with even more business exploits – not all of them favourable.

"Don't worry, Terry, it will all turn out fine," my friend Wayne Peters assured me. There was nothing to do but trust him, because I had no experience at all when it came to fertilisers, sand mines or peat farms, despite suddenly finding myself involved in Amgrow Pty Ltd, a business that involved all three. Wayne is a serious and very clever young man who now runs a successful investment fund, which is why he was able to convince me, along with our dear friend Barry McCollam, to go into business with him. Amgrow Pty Ltd produced fertilisers on a huge scale and came with a 200-acre peat farm and a 200-acre sand mine. For a while, it seemed we had made a big mistake. The first time I walked into the Amgrow factory it was to find hundreds of workers, a massive production line and fertiliser everywhere – I felt we were about to be buried in it! First, the workers went on strike, then the man who sold us the idea was revealed as a con man. It got worse: the government informed us that they weren't going to renew our licence to mine the peat. Thankfully, Wayne managed to sell the factory to one of the biggest fertiliser producers in Australia, which recouped our total outlay and left us the peat mine and sand mine for free. He also challenged the New South Wales Government's decision not to renew our licence, and a public inquiry was convened. Wayne flew in experts from all over the globe as the inquiry dragged on and on, and for nearly nine months we fought those who had objected to our licence renewal. Eventually, the government was forced to concede that they had no grounds for not renewing the licence. Victory was ours and we had a champagne party to celebrate it – but the last laugh was not ours! Soon the government declared the whole area a conservation reserve, decreeing that all industry there must cease. They also decided that, by mining peat, we had contaminated the Sydney water supply and promptly sued us for $30 million. At that point, I decided I wanted nothing more to do with mining or industry of any kind. And I never have. People often ask me what is the secret to business success, and I don't always have an answer. One thing I do know is that every business failure or close call I had taught me as much about business as every success.

THANKS FOR THE MEMORIES

"Grandad!" my grandson James never fails to greet me with a big hug and a kiss, and although he is now happily married to Bryony, his childhood sweetheart, he is still a big part of the lives of Jean and I. He has a passion for watches and has a great career ahead of him with one of Switzerland's leading watchmakers. Like all of my grandchildren, he received part of his education at the excellent Dean Close School in Cheltenham. Being able to pay for my grandchildren's education is just one of the many benefits of achieving the wealth I dreamed of as a young journalist in Dagenham. Like his mother Michelle, my son Terry, and me, James is also a business go-getter, even setting up a chocolate fountain company while still at school. His younger sister Grace is a sensitive young lady who wears her heart on her sleeve. She is still at Dean Close School and looking forward to university She once told me she wanted to be a Commodore on a cruise ship though I had thought that if any of my grandchildren would be interested in following in my footsteps then it would be my eldest granddaughter Gemma, who spent much of her first two years on a cruise liner. Gemma, however, studied midwifery at university and spent her first year out at a maternity hospital in Cornwall. She then gave it all up when she fell in love with a brilliant young scientist and they married and moved to America, where he built a reputation as an expert in cancer research. There's nothing I enjoy more than a cuddle and I am so lucky to have so many beautiful granddaughters who love to snuggle up on the sofa with granddad. Terry's four girls are also different but all so lovable in their own way. Suzannah had a few troubled years before settling down to teach at a Kindergarten in Sheffield and she now seems very settled with her life. Georgina, we see most of, because she now plays a big part in the running of Willoughby House. Gabriella and Amelia are in Australia but flit between the two countries like they are a stone's throw apart. It was wonderful to have my whole family around me when I celebrated my 60th birthday with a big party at Bentham.

Since retiring, it seemed, I had become even busier than I had been when I was working, but I still found time to keep in touch with my old shipmates and invited them along to the party, which we held at Bentham Country Club. I was privileged in that we had many talented entertainers on board our ships over the years, and I was friends with many of them, including one of my favourite singers, Emma Ward. I had watched her blossom from a sweet 19-year-old entertainer into one of the most influential figures in the cruise industry. She sang No Regrets for me, before our former bandleader, Ian Smith, dragged me on stage to do one of my regular party pieces – a poor imitation of Al Jolson.

Later, 'Thanks for the Memory,' crooned my friend Frank Forde, as a humorous conclusion.

Of 60 years today, a long, long time away,
Since Terry looked around him and decided that he'd stay,
Oh thank you, so much,
Thanks for the memory.
Of all the years between, the happy times with Jean,
And then young Michelle and Terry appearing on the scene,
Oh thank you, so much.
He was the boss aboard ship,
He came a long way from the smoke,
I was one act of his choosing. He liked my joke.
Hey what a bloke!
Thanks for the memory,
Of hearing Terry sing,
He likes to do his thing,
He thinks he sounds like Jolson, But I think I sound like Bing,
Oh thank you, so much…
Thanks for the memory.
There's one more thing to say, on this his special day
It's taken 60 years to reach the handicap you play!
Awfully glad I met you, have another swinging year,

Oh thank you, Terry, so much…

He was right about one thing, a lot of time and effort had gone into my golf swing. More than I ever imagined. Although I was always interested in sports, I had never tried golf seriously until I moved to Australia. At Sanctuary Cove, playing golf is almost compulsory and now Jean can also play a round at the course and actually enjoy it. Years before, in Madeira, I had become friendly with British Open Champion Nick Price, and met up with him again when a skins tournament was held at Sanctuary Cove. I went out to watch him play, in the company of other golfing greats like Greg Norman and local champion Ian Baker-Finch, and thought it didn't look all that difficult. Here I am 16 years later trying to develop that elusive swing. I even bought a golf course with Ian and Barry McCollam in the hope that it would help me improve!

My first teacher was Bob Weir, one of Australia's best coaches and the former chairman of the Australian PGA. Bob got me my first handicap of 27 – enough to allow me to enter weekly competitions. It took a while before Bob managed to successfully tweak my swing and drop my handicap to 14. I was pretty pleased with that, on one of Australia's most difficult courses, but then I started going backwards. When I did start to improve again, most of what I learned had little to do with the technicalities of my swing. It didn't help that I was lucky enough to play in the company of world-class golfers such as Greg Norman, Ian Baker-Finch, Peter Senior, Nick Price, Terry Price and Ronan Rafferty. Soon I found myself trying to follow their styles, which was always doomed to failure.

"Golf is a game where you have to try really hard not to try really hard," Ian told me one day. What he meant was that I had to remain soft and supple in the swing and not stiff as a board trying to knock the cover off the ball or imitate someone else. In fact, Ian gave me the best advice I've ever received, and it consisted of just a few words: "You play much better with a smile on your face." It was something I had to remind myself of time and time again when I decided to join him and Barry in purchasing The Glades.

Our venture started in an encouraging way, and The Glades was soon voted the top resort course in Australia. During the time we owned the course I learned a lot about golf, not because I particularly wanted to, but more because I was the only one of the owners based in Australia…and because I had to learn to prevent us from going bankrupt. Originally, I'd intended to be a silent investor, but when Ian moved permanently to Florida to take up a position as a TV presenter, he left a friend in charge of building a new clubhouse and generally looking after the club. I agreed to put my signature on a fixed-price contract to build a lavish clubhouse at a cost of $5 million Australian dollars. The builders, a company called Thakral, were also planning to build around 700 luxury homes around the course, and each time they sold one with a membership to the course they promised to hand over a cheque to us for around $20,000. It seemed like a very good deal when they built their first 100 homes and sold a membership to every single purchaser, meaning they owed us $2 million. Unfortunately, when they hadn't paid us this amount some time later, I arranged a meeting with their English boss to ask where the money was.

"I'm sorry but the cost of the clubhouse has run over budget," he informed me. "Actually, by more than that amount. So, in fact, you owe us money."

I soon found out that all sorts of underhand activities were going on, including people playing on the course for free. Pretty soon we had to prop up the venture with more cash, and I felt like I had no alternative but to be there to keep an eye on things, and Barry agreed. Unfortunately, Ian thought I was interfering. I quickly installed a new general manager, David White, who changed our fortunes dramatically and we soon turned a corner. Still, I was relieved when, sometime soon after, a wealthy Chinese purchaser arrived and we avoided what could have been a potential business embarrassment.

Now, I remain a member of The Pines and The Palms at Sanctuary Cove, and until he became too frail to play, enjoyed an occasional game on the exclusive Villa private course with the late Max Bygraves. I had known Max almost all my life, although for many years he remained unaware of that fact. He used to sing for just three quid a night at a local pub in Dagenham, the Merry Fiddlers, when I was just a boy, before anyone realised what a colossal star he would later become. Later, when Max became a star performer, every Christmas (as it was for many British households) we Hopleys used to invite him into our house via his records and sing along with Max, belting out 'You Need Hands' and 'Fings Ain't Wot They Used t'Be' and all of his other classic hits. I never imagined that I would get the chance to sing along with Max in person, but his friendship was a great gift and I saw him nearly every day when I was in Australia. Because Max travelled so much, he was a frequent visitor at the Hyatt in Singapore. When he moved to Australia, the Hyatt did not forget his patronage. The manager of the Singapore Hyatt called the Hyatt at Sanctuary Cove to remind them to arrange a birthday cake for Max on his birthday. As we were also dining at the Hyatt on the same day, the manager introduced us, thinking that, as we were all English, we would no doubt have much to talk about. We sure did, quickly discovering the Dagenham connection, and spent hours chatting (and singing) on the terrace of his beautiful home. It's marvellous to remember that my good mate received an OBE, once supported Judy Garland, and had more than fifty hit records. He appeared in several films, and was one of the Queen's favourite Royal Variety Show performers! To coin a phrase of Max's, his friendship really made me stop sometimes and think, 'I've arrived—and to prove it, I'm here!' Both he and his lovely wife Blossom died within a year of each other but only a short time before they paid Jean and I a lovely compliment when they told us that, although we had not been friends for long, they considered us their very best friends.

"What do you mean we haven't been friends for long?" I responded, "We had you in our house for Christmas for nearly fifty years. You just didn't realise I was your friend!"

I am also a member of Royal Mougins in France and Loch Lomond in Scotland but membership of so many world-class golf courses has not done much for my handicap and I know only too well there is always room for improvement. Mind you, this may ruffle some feathers, but it is my opinion that courses in Australia are tougher for the average golfer than those in the UK, and I can prove it. Recently, Pat and Ainsley Hewitt, close friends from Essex, moved to Sanctuary Cove. Ainsley was always a useful golfer and in his younger days he even got down to single figures. When he departed England two years ago, his handicap at Orsett Golf Club in Essex was twelve. He duly put in his five cards for a handicap here at The Pines and played to 23. Despite playing twice a week since then, he has only managed to drop a couple of shots. I know a lot of my English friends will defend golf in the UK by citing the championship courses, but I am talking about the usual members' course. They will also say that the English weather makes the game that much tougher, and while it is absolutely true that Australians don't play in the rain and biting cold, neither do I. Why would we when we have more than 300 sunny days a year? Without exception my mates from the UK, even dedicated golfers, have been murdered by the sixteen lakes that dominate The Pines. One year, my good friends Alan Ball and Roger Hunt (both members of England's famous world-cup winning football side) came out to Australia to visit. They found The Pines a very tough proposition. Alan played golf the way he used to play football. He gave 150 per cent and woe betide you if you didn't hit the form he expected of you. Mind you, he was also great fun to play with. Alan had a name for every shot. A shot that doesn't leave the ground is called a Barbara Streisand (ugly, but still working). A mis-hit shot that has a few lucky bounces to finish where you intended he calls a sister-in-law (you're up there, but you know you shouldn't be) and a tricky little putt is an Alan Ball (a nasty five footer). His nickname for me was Bing (straight down the middle), even though on some occasions I was in the trees more than I was in the fairways. We played with Geoff partnering Roger, and me partnering Alan, and for the duration of my friends' stay we made it a habit that the winners would choose where we went to dinner that evening – and the losers had to pay. On one particular game during which I spent most of my time in the trees, we were beaten by Geoff and Roger, who gleefully chose the most magnificent seafood restaurant they could think of for dinner with the that evening. The restaurant is called Omeros Brothers, so I rang to make a reservation to ensure we got a table that overlooked the ocean. The owner was a football nut and was beside himself to hear that three of the England forward line from the 1966 World Cup final were coming to his restaurant.

"I've got a proposal for you," he told me enthusiastically. "If I can get a football for tonight, do you think you could get the boys to sign it so we can auction it for charity. Of course, in return, your meals will be on the house and we'll be sure to give you a night to remember," he promised.

I could see this turning into a great joke for me, and a way for our losing team to make good. "No problem," I told him.

Omeros Brothers lived up to the owner's word. We dined sumptuously on lobster, prawns, and that wonderful Australian delicacy, Moreton Bay Bug, all washed down with the finest of wines. All throughout dinner, Roger and Geoff were delighted that the hefty bill was coming the way of Alan and me and made numerous jokes about our predicament. Once we had all had a few glasses of excellent wine, I produced the football.

"The owner is a great football fan," I told them, "and he'd like you to sign this ball for his cancer charity."

Of course, all of them are used to being asked for their autographs and regularly participate in charity events and they readily agreed to sign the ball.

"Thanks boys," I said before the ink was even dry, "that's the tab taken care of."

It was a long time before my friends let me forget it, but the owner, Nick Omeros, was delighted. The ball raised $6000 for his charity when it was auctioned a few weeks later.

Another of my charity efforts was far less successful. My daughter Michelle is heavily involved in church and charity work and one of her regular commitments is helping to cook for the needy at the local church hall. In winter they also provide warm second-hand clothing and other pre-loved goods for the less fortunate.

"You've got a mountain of clothes you never wear," my daughter cornered me one day when I was in Cheltenham. "Just sort out the things you don't wear and bring them down on Friday lunchtime and we'll give them to the homeless," she encouraged me. "It's so touching to see a homeless person choosing something warm to wear."

So I sorted out all of my sweaters, shirts and jackets and dutifully took them all down to the church hall the following Friday.

"Just leave them on that table over there," Michelle instructed. "They'll come over and help themselves."

I left my pile of clothes on the table and sat back, ready to be touched by the spectacle of homeless people benefiting from my cast offs. But I couldn't believe it when the first lady who came in, pushing a dilapidated empty pram, scooped up the whole lot with a gleeful grin. I certainly did get to see a homeless person choosing something warm to wear – but only 'a' homeless person! The next week I walked down The Promenade and saw the same unkempt lady, still pushing her battered pram but this time wearing a £150 Paul and Shark sweater.

ACHES AND PAINS

To thank you for your wonderful assistance during Jean's period of illness, Jean and Terry Hopley would like to invite you to dinner at Willoughby House. Menu:

To Start

Cornish lobster (anaesthetised by James de Courcy)

Main

Roast rib of beef (hand carved by orthopaedic surgeon Guy Rooker)

Dessert

Half an Ogen melon topped with a glazed cherry (personal selection of gynaecologist David Holmes)

When Jean required a hysterectomy a few years ago, I decided to thank the wonderful medical team who assisted her recovery by inviting them to a special dinner at the wonderful hotel, Willoughby House. Of course, as I had learned with my back troubles, it's never wise to go into any medical procedure lightly. Even though we were living in Australia at the time, I chose Cheltenham consultant David Holmes to perform the operation at Nuffield Hospital in the UK. David and his wife Liz are now among our closest friends. Jean's operation went smoothly enough and she was home within a week, but within a few days she began to suffer severe pains in the pelvic area. Such pains often disappear within a day or two with bed rest, she was told, but Jean's pains rapidly became much worse. When she collapsed, I quickly rushed her to hospital and she was re-admitted and remained there for four months, first at Nuffield and then in a special wing of Cheltenham General Hospital. However, the cause of her intense pain remained a mystery.

A number of specialists tried to locate the problem, and David was a daily visitor to Jean's bedside, as, of course, was I. By Christmas, Jean's condition was deteriorating. She was in such pain she could no longer get out of bed and, in spite of the many tests and experiments with different antibiotics, nothing seemed to work. At around that time, I stopped being a daily visitor, and became a patient myself! I suffered a very painful bout of shingles and ended up spending the Christmas holidays admitted to the room next door to Jean.

"Terry, I wanted to come and let you know that I think we will need to operate on Jean again," David visited my bedside on Boxing Day. "The only way of trying to find out just what's causing the pain is to reopen the wound. It may be that there is a problem in the pelvic bone, so I plan to operate together with an orthopaedic surgeon."

"Then you must use Guy Rooker, a surgeon I know," I insisted. Guy had many years of experience and I trusted him. The next day, David drove around to Guy's house to ask if he would give up some of his Christmas holidays to come and operate on my wife, and to his credit, he said yes. On the day of the operation, Terry and I waited nervously outside the operating theatre.

"Terry," Guy was the first out of the theatre. "You'll be relieved to hear that we found the problem immediately. When we drilled an experimental hole in the pelvic bone, a lot of pus burst out. Jean has an infection in her pelvis. It was analysed and we have determined that it is pseudomonas. It's not an uncommon infection, but it is unknown following a gynaecological procedure."

My wife looked pale and exhausted when they wheeled her back into her room, but her recovery from that point on was swift and she was home within a couple of weeks. I was so relieved to see Jean well again that I thought I would thank the staff who had looked after her with such care.

"I'm thinking of having a dinner at Willoughby House to thank the staff," I told the sister. "Can you please send a note around to see how many people would like to come?"

When the note was returned to me, there were more than 50 names on it, including both surgeons and anaesthetist James de Courcy, and I was extremely happy to be able to entertain them all at Willoughby House. I am sure they enjoyed it too.

As one of my most successful business acquisitions, Willoughby House Hotel, in Suffolk Square, Cheltenham, was the logical place for such a celebration. It had come into my family business portfolio almost by accident.

"Dad, did you see Willoughby House is for sale?" Terry had quizzed me one morning. "It's on the market for the first time in a hundred years. We could really turn that place into something."

I had to agree with him. Willoughby House is the finest regency townhouse in Cheltenham and was converted into a hotel when the previous owner could no longer afford to maintain it as a private residence. The lady who owned it was 76 and had been born and raised in the house. It was desperately in need of renovation and when we first inspected it we were appalled to see linoleum on the floors and paper tablecloths on the table. But the potential of this elegant, heritage-listed building shone though. It cost a small fortune to restore to its former glory, but it was worth every penny. It is now a landmark hotel in Cheltenham and the surrounding gardens have won 'Cheltenham in Bloom' floral awards six times. The hotel soon became such a success that we acquired another regency building, Elizabeth House, nearby, which offers classic self-contained apartments in conjunction with the hotel. The renovations were difficult, but by far the most difficult part of running Willoughby House was finding suitable managers. Our first managers seemed capable and efficient to start with – until we learned that when we weren't around they often went out and left the hotel in the hands of guests, telling them, "Just help yourselves to whatever you want from the bar or the kitchen."

We replaced them immediately with another couple, who interviewed well but were sent on their way after just one day. When the man asked me: "Is it okay if I smoke in the public areas, and can I take a bottle of gin from the bar back to my apartment?" I thought it best to send them packing. The next young couple almost put us out of business. He was a qualified chef who regularly featured 'blue soup' on the menu and she was a surly woman who often didn't appear until nearly lunchtime. We bid them a hasty farewell, too. I'm not sure what it is about hotel managers, perhaps it was the Basil Fawlty effect, but almost all of our managers in those early days were hopeless. The next manager was a former Royal Naval officer.

"No need to worry about me, sir, I had full responsibility for looking after the Ward Room for the Admiral," he told us proudly at the interview. Poor admiral! Our new manager vanished from midday everyday for a 'sales meeting' and returned late in the afternoon worse for wear, only to sleep it off in the guest lounge. He, too, got the push. Our next managers put my mind at ease…for a while. They started out brilliantly, but, oddly, it wasn't long before our sales figures started to drop.

"My apartment is quite simply not up to the standard of the rest of the hotel and I want a refund or a room change," an American guest demanded one day. As our apartments at Elizabeth House were equally as impressive as the hotel rooms at Willoughby House, we were a little puzzled by his problem.

"Well, sir, if you'd like to take me there and show me what's wrong, I'll happily resolve it for you," I told him. The American took me to his 'apartment', which was indeed dirty and scruffy with peeling wallpaper on the walls – it was also not in Elizabeth House! On looking into it, we discovered that our new manager had a criminal record for fraud and was diverting our customers to a couple of shoddy little apartments he had acquired down the road. Another manager bit the dust. So much for my retirement, it seemed I was doing as much as I had when I was still working!

In desperation, I called on one of the most efficient operators I had ever met – my former 'commodore-in-waiting' Sarah Lloyd. She was brilliant at her job, spoke several languages and solved problems with consummate ease…she also acted like she owned the place. However, Sarah was so good at her job that she soon had the hotel shipshape and meeting the high standards I required. As she had with the ships, she quickly had the hotel operating to near 100 per cent capacity. Once Sarah had everything under control, which didn't take her very long, she decided that instead of coming in to work every day, she would simply pop in when it suited her, just like I did. She was that good, that she probably would have got away with it, but she soon fell pregnant with her second baby and resigned, leaving us looking for a new manager. She now lives in Spain with her husband and I am sure that whatever she is doing, she is doing it splendidly, and upsetting a few people in the process.

"It's just so difficult to find good managerial staff," I complained to Geoff and Judith Hurst one night over dinner at Poachers in Winchcombe, one of my favourite Cotswold restaurants. The food and standards at Poachers were always excellent and I desperately needed a similar level of catering at Willoughby.

"I just don't know how we're going to manage?" I moaned again as I handed over the bill and my card to Clare Eckerman, the wife of chef and owner Frank.

"If you two ever think of leaving here, don't do anything without thinking of me first," I told her.

"Actually, we might be interested," Clare responded. "We've been talking about the possibility of selling the restaurant."

I arranged to meet with Clare and Frank for an informal interview the next day, and within a month our new managers were firmly installed. They spent seven years running the hotel and Willoughby House became a business I could be truly proud of. I was happy to celebrate my seventieth birthday there. If you are ever in Cheltenham, look it up, but be sure to make reservations early, as it is frequently booked out. Frank finally decided to call it a day through ill-health and my old ship-mate Emma Ward came to the rescue by taking over as manager temporarily. Then, following the break-up of his 20-year marriage, Terry Junior returned to the UK with his beautiful partner Vanessa and they have taken Willoughby House to even greater heights.

SANCTUARIES

Of course, Jean's illness hasn't been the only medical drama that has required attention, and I guess another inevitable factor in our decision where to spend the majority of our golden years is healthcare. As Jean and I grow older, it would be foolish of us not to consider which country has the best medical facilities, although the jury is still out on that one.

While Jean was ill, her discomfort and the many natural therapies she trialled gave me another business idea. Perhaps it was ahead of its time, but, unfortunately, it was a business that has to be placed on the list of disappointments rather than achievements. Jean had enjoyed having manicures, pedicures and aromatherapy massages, as well as trying other natural therapies to improve her condition and to help her relax and feel better while she was ill. We came up with the idea of a luxurious health suite, where patients could enjoy relaxing or nurturing therapies at the same time as attending to other medical problems. Figuring it would do better in England than in Australia, I bought a five-storey building in the centre of Cheltenham and set about turning it into a health sanctuary. The health suite contained a small gymnasium and twelve treatment rooms, and it offered everything from Indian head massage to endermology (a new and very expensive treatment for cellulite), as well as gynaecological and other appointments. David Holmes set up a consulting room for his private practice and we had other consultants waiting in the wings. When someone is ill, the last thing they want is to be in depressing surrounds, so we tried to make it as luxurious as possible, with exquisite furniture and fittings and waiting rooms where patients were served tea and biscuits on Royal Doulton China while they waited. It seemed like an excellent way to brighten up the day of patients and provide a one-stop shop when it came to making appointments, but, strangely, it didn't work and within a year we closed it and sold the building.

You may think the idea was a bit ambitious, and it probably was, although I am sure it would do better now than it did when we conceived it almost ten years ago. After all, health spas and retreats are far more common than they were then. But perhaps I was wrong in basing it in the UK. Jean and I, along with Geoff and Judith Hurst, recently visited The Golden Door, a luxurious health retreat in the Hunter Valley of New South Wales. While it doesn't provide medical services, it combines exercise, such as Tai Chi, bushwalking, dancing and deepwater running, with relaxing luxury treatments and health lectures. There is certainly nothing like The Golden Door in the UK, so perhaps my idea was not the problem, perhaps I just based it in the wrong country. The health suite was also not my most ambitious business effort – that distinction is reserved for a venture that was so ambitious it didn't even come off.

Sanctuary Cove, our home in Australia, is an exclusive gated community on the Gold Coast in Queensland. I bought our house there because I couldn't imagine a place that offered better weather or a greater number of opportunities to enjoy one's self in any given day. In fact, I am lucky enough that at Sanctuary Cove I don't even have to leave the community to enjoy any number of activities. As an example, a typical day at home in Sanctuary Cove might entail driving my golf buggy down to any one of a dozen small local restaurants for breakfast, where I might run into any number of good friends and numerous local celebrities. Although, if I fancy something healthy and want to eat at home, I can always prepare it myself and sit outside in the morning sun for most of the year (even if I have to share my breakfast with exquisite rainbow lorikeets, which frequent the mock orange trees in our garden). It's just a short stroll to the gym and tennis courts, or I can enjoy a game of golf on one of two championship golf courses right on my doorstep. If I am not up to a full game, well the practice balls are stacked in neat little triangles just waiting for a hit. I can take a dip in our pool or visit the village shops. To visit many of my friends, I simply walk down to our private jetty and hop on to my motor cruiser to ride over to their home in the harbour or on the Coomera River. I may even take the cruiser out to explore one of the nearby sand islands or beaches – all of this within a few kilometres of home. However, even the best-planned resorts can struggle if they are not properly managed, and Sanctuary Cove was no exception. When we learned that Sanctuary Cove was in receivership, a group of us, led, of course, by the brilliant Wayne Peters formed a consortium to buy it for around $210 million. We really believed we had a good chance of success, and, after my experience at running The Glades, I was particularly excited about getting a chance to better manage the golf courses (and all that went with them). However, in retrospect, I can understand that we really had little chance at all. Unfortunately for us, the receiver had the task of nominating the successful bidder and he chose a little known Malaysian company called Mulpha, who, in my opinion, picked up an absolute bargain and went on to double its money in just three years. Sanctuary Cove is full of residents far cleverer than I and looking back I find it hard to believe that we didn't organise ourselves sufficiently well to become the owners of our own world-beating residential community. Mulpha later asked me to become the president of the Sanctuary Cove Country Club. I didn't accept, but agreed to become vice president for the rest of the year, during which time a new company was structured, with each member becoming a shareholder. A few alarming business plans were put forward and I gracefully made my exit, declining the invitation to put myself forward as the next president.

Although it is easy for me to expound the many benefits of life in Australia, my family most definitely don't agree. They have all had long periods living in Queensland but all are now happily settled back in the Cotswolds and that is where I can see us spending our twilight years. The cost of living in Australia is no longer lower than that of England, and although the weather makes a tremendous difference when it comes to lifestyle we can fly to our home on the French Riviera in a couple of hours. Australia is probably less plagued by the lack of commonsense that England has experienced when it comes to political correctness, although I can see it is following in Britain's footsteps. Recently, when Jean and I flew from London Heathrow to holiday in Bahrain at Christmas time, Heathrow was devoid of any Christmas cheer. Some decision-maker had thought decorations might cause offence. The airport security was also beset by a kind of prejudicial procedure that seemed hard to fathom. Of course, everybody needs to feel secure when they are boarding a plane, but the level of security was ludicrous – if only because it didn't apply to everyone. While we had to remove our coats, jewellery, belts and shoes before going through the x-ray machine, others who were directly ahead of us and for reasons of their faith were wearing long, flowing garments were not required to remove any items of clothing. It did seem farcical to see my senior citizen wife barefoot and being frisked while masked women passed through unchallenged. Travelling first class with Gulf Air turned out to be incredibly opulent. The seats reclined into a flat bed, the gracious hostesses provided pyjamas for when you felt tired, and there was even an onboard chef who could prepare and serve anything you required at any time. However, I was even more impressed when we arrived in Bahrain. The first thing that greeted us in this Muslim country was the Christmas carol 'Jingle Bells' floating over the PA system. We queued up to get into the country with the line winding its way past a huge, illuminated Father Christmas directly outside the customs area.

"What have the PC brigade done to my beautiful England?" I thought later that night as Jean and I enjoyed a fabulous Mexican meal in the restaurant of our lovely Bahrain hotel. Outside a choir of children sang 'O' Come All Ye Faithful' and afterwards Father Christmas made a special appearance and each child sat on his knee to receive a present. There was not a protest from the primarily Muslim residents. In fact, the feeling of friendship and goodwill was far more evident than in any London hotel I have been in recently. It made me even more convinced that the wrong people are running, and ruining, Britain. I have met a lot of politicians in my day, but I am yet to meet one who could run a piss-up in a brewery. Like all old people, I can tell you it was not like that in my day. However, many of my family and friends remain in England, and they will always be the magnet that draws me towards the country of my birth. 'Family comes first', my father always taught me, and that certainly applies to me as far as my children and grandchildren are concerned. I am thankful that I am fortunate enough to be able to enjoy both countries, moving between Europe and Australia regularly enough to see all my grandchildren grow up.

BACK AT SEA

"Wait! Now, where on earth are my glasses," Judith groaned as she rummaged through her handbag in the back seat of my Lexus land cruiser, which was already packed to the brim with luggage for our holiday.

"We'll check the house," I said, rolling my eyes. Jean and I frantically searched the house again, while Geoff and Terry Jnr, who was to drive us to the cruise ship terminal, rummaged through the car. Apart from Terry, who was driving us to the terminal, we were all setting off to return to the UK via the P&O flagship MV *Aurora*. We would be travelling from Brisbane to Southampton via Darwin, Singapore, Vietnam, Japan, Honolulu, San Francisco, Mexico, Panama, Aruba, Barbados and the Azores. Even with that packed itinerary, Geoff and I could hardly believe the amount of luggage lined up to take onboard. Our convoy was made even more cumbersome by an enormous, two-metre long oil on canvas painting of Geoff scoring his 'They Think It's All Over' goal, which required a separate, specially hired truck to transport it onto the ship. When Terry moved to Australia, his best friend Rob Campion and Rob's wife Gill moved to Australia too. Gill is a very talented artist and when she saw a photograph of Geoff scoring the final of his world-cup-winning goals, she said she would like to do an oil on canvas from the photo. She did an excellent job and Geoff was thrilled with it, but none of us had quite considered that she planned it for a canvas so large. I had called the *Aurora* and asked if it was okay if we brought it onboard and they had, thankfully, agreed. Meanwhile, our search for Judith's glasses was continuing without much success.

"Maybe you packed them," Jean suggested after we had searched the house for about half an hour. We all began searching whatever bags were easy to get to, until Terry Jnr looked at Geoff and said, "Why are you wearing Judith's spectacles?"

Geoff had been wearing them the entire time – even though his prescription is nothing like Judith's and he can barely see through them!

"Why does it always seem like an outing from an old folks home with you lot?" Terry grinned. Nevertheless, we made it aboard on time and with all spectacles accounted for.

It would be easy enough for me to fly from continent to continent, travelling first class, but old habits die hard, and most of the time I travel by sea. I don't cruise just for nostalgia's sake, but because I genuinely enjoy it more than flying. Many people who have never cruised have expressed to me their belief that if the weather were inclement there would be nothing to do on board. They could not be further from the truth. Aboard the MV *Aurora*, GI Geoff, the exercise freak, began our days with an hour long walk around the top deck. The GI stands for glycaemic index, a subject my health-conscious mate is an expert in, although I have to admit that he is incredibly fit and is not far off his playing weight when he led England to victory all those years ago. We would all then enjoy a leisurely and healthy breakfast around the Crystal Pool, which has a sliding glass roof in case of rain. Mid-morning we were able to attend lectures by invited guests and speakers. I attended one by a human-behaviour expert who had spent more than 400 hours interviewing Peter Sutcliffe, the 'Yorkshire Ripper', and another one called 'Life Below Decks' (although the latter did seem to repeat a lot of stories I have heard before and are possibly 'old ship's tales'). If we fancied something different we could choose between a game on a golf simulator, taking part in a trivia quiz, playing a seven-a-side cricket match, going to dance classes, learning to play bridge, taking a French language class or having a computer lesson. If none of those appealed, we could also choose to sit quietly and read in one of the many warm, sheltered sites on one of the decks. One morning, as I was doing just that (and actually berating myself for not having put in a few chapters on this book the day before), I came across a passage that was to take a huge weight off my mind. I was reading a book called *Humble Pie*, the autobiography of notorious TV chef Gordon Ramsay. I quite like to marvel at the successes and failures people have had in life (and obviously you do too or you wouldn't be reading this book), and I admire people like Gordon, who like me, worked his way from a poor upbringing to a life of luxury. As I was reading it, I suddenly began to chuckle. The chuckle soon grew to a laugh and had Jean wondering what was so funny. I had come to a section in which Gordon was describing his violent and aggressive father. The book went on to mention an incident in which his dad and sister, who were musicians, were thrown off a cruise ship in Corfu. It did not take me long to realise that the angry guitarist I thought had fallen foul of George's hitmen was actually Gordon Ramsay's dad! George's assassin could not have found him after all, but he probably never realised what a lucky escape he had. Personally, I could not have been more relieved to know that the terrible guilt I had lived with for years was all in my head.

Travelling by cruise ship also gives me a chance to reflect on the many differences between cruise ships now and those back in my days. I had told myself I would devote a large part of the cruise to finishing this book, but that was before I realised I had forgotten my laptop charger, which put my plans on hold. I requested that the charger be posted to meet the ship in Singapore, and informed the ship's purser to expect it from the ship's agent. Unfortunately, it didn't arrive in Singapore, so I splashed out and bought a new Sony Vaio instead, although the purser assured me that my parcel would be sent on to meet the ship when we arrived in Hong Kong. Of course, it wasn't there, which didn't help with my first impression of the staff. When we had first boarded the *Aurora*, thinking that the captain and I probably had a lot in common, I left a message at reception that I would love to have a cup of tea with him. However, despite leaving many messages, almost one a day for the first two weeks, I heard nothing from him. It didn't help when we were also contacted by the staff to tell us that, despite earlier approval to have the painting stowed on board, it was now found to be against their insurance policy.

"If it were to be damaged in the hold, it could be problematic," we were told.

"But it's not valuable," I argued. "Don't get me wrong, it is a beautiful piece of art, but a friend painted it personally for Geoff Hurst. In fact, it was a gift and cost nothing." My arguments came to nothing and we ended up with the painting stashed between the couch and the wall in our cabin. It was a bit rich, I thought, because, before we had even boarded the *Aurora*, our two-month holiday turned into a bit of a promotional gig for P&O. As soon as the staff realised Sir Geoff Hurst was joining the ship, they persuaded him to give a few talks and take part in a question and answer session. Of course, Geoff gets recognised just about wherever he is, and with around 2000 Brits on board, it didn't take long for word to spread that Sir Geoff Hurst was on the *Aurora*. Within days he was being invited to countless dinners and drinks with other guests, all of which he refused. Geoff has become quite used to having followers wherever he goes, and, for the most part, he puts up with his fan club with good grace, even when it becomes tiring. I am amazed at his patience, even when a fan approaches halfway through a meal and dominates the conversation for half an hour. I get more fed up with it than Geoff does, but that could be because I would rather be the centre of attention! On the *Aurora* it often meant super-fit Geoff had to speed up on his morning fast walk around the promenade deck, just to lose unfit and unwelcome hangers-on who accosted him daily as he exercised. He was more popular than the captain – and no doubt talked to more people!

At that stage, I was still wondering why I hadn't heard back from Captain Ian Walters. Of course, Geoff's popularity onboard the ship soon provided the perfect solution to getting the enormous painting out of my cabin.

"There's been a lot of interest in Geoff Hurst on the ship," I informed the cruise director. "Judging by the number of people who stop Geoff for a chat, perhaps we could exhibit the painting of him scoring the final goal in the atrium for a few days. We would be happy to let you have it to display, as long as it can be wrapped in bubble wrap and returned to the hold for safekeeping afterwards."

The cruise director readily agreed. "Great! We'll advertise his talk and the showing in the entertainment programme," he told me. Geoff is one of the most famous sportsman on the planet, but that doesn't seem to stop people regularly getting his name wrong and spelling it Jeff Hurst, Geoff Hirst of even Jeff Hirst. I also knew a bit about cruise directors and guessed that if I did not go down there and give them the exact wording for the painting, anything could go in the programme.

"Ok, so we're all clear that it should read: Sir Geoff Hurst MBE – that's G...E...O...F...F ... H...U...R...S...T – scoring the final goal of the 1966 World Cup, in which England beat Germany 4–2."

"Yes, yes. Got it!" I was told. The next day, when the painting went on display it was with the correct caption: 'Sir Geoff Hurst, scoring the final goal of the 1966 World Cup, in which England beat Germany 4–2.' Followed by:

'Painted by fellow passenger and artist Terry Hopley.'

Geoff is very professional around his many fans, but in private he can be an absolute scream. When we are cruising, it doesn't take long before he starts playing practical joke on the stewards and waiters, hiding their vacuum cleaners or stealing all their bars of soap. Despite this, waiters always go out of their way to please him, bringing him double portions of dessert that end up making us all a little overweight. I am sure it is Geoff's extra servings that have led to his nickname for me – 'fatso'! While sometimes fame can have its advantages, most of the time I am sure Geoff would just like to enjoy his holiday in peace. Last year, when Geoff, Judith, Jean and I cruised around New Zealand on the *Silver Shadow*, I got a taste of just what that level of fame was like – well, almost. You see, Geoff believes that I go around telling everyone who he is, and I have to admit that I sometimes do.

"Don't do that, Terry. It's so embarrassing," he'll groan when I've introduced him to someone as 'Sir Geoff Hurst MBE'.

"Nonsense," I would reply. "If I were Geoff Hurst I would be delighted if everyone knew me and asked for my autograph."

"Oh no, you wouldn't," Geoff responded. "You'd hate it, and I'm going to prove it to you."

"Excuse me," he tapped the shoulder of a perfect stranger standing nearby. "Do you know who this is?"

The stranger threw a blank stare in my direction.

"This is Commodore Terry Hopley," Geoff continued enthusiastically. "The Commodore Terry Hopley. He used to be the editor-in-chief of Greater London and Essex Newspapers, then he was the chairman of Fourwinds Cruises. Made a fortune chartering cruise ships he did, and he knows more about cruising than anyone in the business. I can't believe you don't know who he is."

By now, his poor victim was nodding hesitantly, trying to pretend they had some idea of who I was.

"Oh stop it, Geoff!" I ordered. But everywhere we went on board Geoff would approach bewildered Americans and expound on my greatness. He was right: it was embarrassing.

"Please, please stop it!" I begged.

"Ok, but only if you solemnly promise you'll never do that to me again," Geoff suggested with a smile.

"I solemnly promise," I told him.

However, it turns out there's one thing I never have to introduce Geoff to: trouble. It seems to follow him around. After one of Geoff's talks on the *Aurora*, while he was busily autographing England shirts and photographs, his wife Judith was approached by one of the other passengers.

"I've noticed you're travelling with Geoff Hurst," the lady pointed towards the stage for Judith's benefit. "Have you seen Rose around the ship?"

"Rose?" Judith queried, "I'm sorry, who is Rose?"

"Rose Hurst," the lady continued. "She is married to Geoff Hurst. She is here, on the *Aurora*, with him."

"I'm afraid you must be mistaken. I am Judith Hurst and I have been married to Geoff Hurst for more than 40 years now," Judith politely corrected her.

"Oh no!" the woman was unconvinced. "She's a friend of mine and she has ALWAYS told me that SHE is married to Geoff Hurst. Her name is Rose Hurst."

It takes all sorts, as they say.

As our cruise continued on, I finally got to visit the bridge. The tour was conducted by a young third officer, and although the captain made a brief appearance, he did not stop to pass the time of day, which I found very disappointing. The bridge had a lot of new equipment, but did not seem to have changed that much since my day otherwise, but then again, what do I know, perhaps my sea-going skills have become a little rusty. Geoff would certainly think so if our holiday on Bedarra Island the year before was taken into account. The tropical island of Bedarra houses Australia's most exclusive resort and we had certainly made the most of it. One day we even borrowed a small motorboat and set off in search of a deserted beach somewhere around the headland. We probably should not have gone out at all really because it was bit choppy and it was not long before the girls became a little frightened.

"Don't worry, girls, I know what I'm doing," I reassured them. At least I thought I knew what I was doing! We soon found a sheltered little spot and, as we had two anchors, I decided that we would drop one about ten metres from the beach, then run the boat up onto the sand and dig the other one into the beach. That would allow us to keep the boat nice and straight in the wind.

"Geoff, grab that anchor," I instructed, "and get ready to drop it over the side."

Too late. Geoff had grabbed it and dropped it over the side in the same movement – about 30 metres from where I'd intended.

"Don't worry about it. Sit down," I said, "Hopefully we'll just drag it along to where we want it."

The anchor took hold when we were literally within two metres from the beach and I thought that was probably just about right. After all, this was where my experience came into play. I peered over the side, judging the water to be only a couple of feet deep.

"Step ashore will you, Geoff, and get ready to plant the second anchor up there." I pointed. Geoff dutifully picked up the anchor and stepped over the side. With a gigantic splash, Geoff was gone – all we could see was his hat as it vanished beneath the waves. A moment later he reappeared, coughing and spluttering.

"Why do I get all the shit jobs?" he asked, staring straight at me. My ability to guess water depth might have become a little rusty, but when it comes to running cruise ships, I have to say I think I've still got the touch. While the *Aurora* is a beautiful ship, certainly much nicer and more modern than any ship I worked on, it somehow lacks personality. We rarely saw officers around the ship, and when we did we usually received little more than a courteous nod. I am sure the British officers are all very professional, but they could certainly do with some public relations training. Cruise ships are often jokingly called 'God's waiting rooms' because of the advanced age of many of the passengers, and the *Aurora* was no different. Having said that, I guess I should not make too many generalizations because we did sit close to a charming elderly couple, George and Phyllis, in the dining room most nights. George was 94 and Phyllis 89, but they were both done up to the nines as they sat enjoying a four-course meal. For the entire cruise, these two young-at-heart seniors never missed a show.

"We do a world cruise every year," Phyllis told us.

"And we enjoy it so much," added George, "Apart from just one thing…"

"Too many old fogies on board!" Phyllis whispered conspiratorially to us, behind her hand, with a giggle.

As the *Aurora* sailed on, somewhere in the North China sea I finally met Captain Ian Walters. I had expected to be disappointed, given that my messages had gone unanswered for so long, but I was pleasantly surprised. He and his lovely wife Vivian accompanied Jean, Geoff, Judith and me for lunch and we found out that we did indeed have something in common, including our desire to spend more time in Australia, and also our wedding anniversary on the 27th June.

"You and Vivian ought to dine at the Columbe D'Or restaurant in St Paul de Vence on your wedding anniversary. It's wonderful," I told Captain Walters, who was due to be in command of the *Arcadia* by then, which was to anchor off Cannes. "You may even run into Jean and I. We should be in the South of France at the same time and we usually go there for lunch on our wedding anniversary."

THESE DAYS

"Shit," Geoff's expletive drifted out to the terrace, closely following the sound of the sugar bowl smashing on the ceramic floor. My mate George turned towards the kitchen, raising an eyebrow as Geoff pottered around cleaning up the mess.

"That's why he was a striker not a goalkeeper," I remarked, but we both knew that Geoff was never just 'a striker'. He's also my mate Geoff, not the legend, not the Geoff who scored 250 goals at the top level of the game, but a character I've known for more than 50 years. Of course, my mate George, who was sitting with us overlooking the beauty of the French Riviera, was no novice with a football either. With more than 800 games for Dagenham FC and two Wembley appearances, George Dudley and Geoff Hurst put my footwork to shame. However, it was more than football that kept us together through the years, and it was much more than football that got us here – relaxing on the terrace of our beautiful home on the Royal Mougins Golf Course in France. Geoff returned with the tea and we sat for a moment in companionable silence. Not a bad lot for senior citizens, I thought, glancing at my mates. Sure we were all a little battle worn, and the good looks and blonde hair that once won George first pick of the ladies had faded to a rugged, completely bald charm, but he is still incredibly fit, recently completing his 19th London Marathon, which added to the many thousands of pounds he has raised for charity. He has gained hardly any pounds on his slim frame, which made me feel slightly guilty about the lasagne to be followed by crème brûlée I had planned for lunch – GI Geoff had to return to the UK for two personal appearances and an autograph-signing session, allowing George and I to indulge. At any rate, I thought, looking over my talented mates, at least I can now hold my own on the golf course, where George and Geoff can both be counted on to lose a dozen of so balls whenever we play 18 holes.

Once Geoff and Judith had said their goodbyes, George and I spent the rest of the evening washing down our meal with a bottle of wine and reminiscing about another of our mates. You see Terry Higgins, Max Bygraves, Dudley Moore, Geoff Hurst, George Dudley and myself were not the only ones to go on from the streets of Essex and the East End to bigger, better things. Another friend, named 'Georgie' (so named to avoid confusing him with George Dudley) was also a Dagenham success story. Back when we were kids, Georgie was just another scruffy urchin we roamed the streets with. He had kicked a ball around with the rest of us, swearing a bit much and displaying the kind of cockney cockiness that saw us getting up to things I probably shouldn't mention, if only not to give the kids these days more ideas of how to be obnoxious. Unfortunately, we lost touch with Georgie after he left Bifrons Secondary Modern, but it's fair to say that he didn't exactly fade into obscurity. His stellar career certainly put our achievements to shame.

"The Archbishop of Canterbury!" can you believe it, laughed George, and I have to admit, I almost couldn't. That Lord Carey – as our childhood mate Georgie is now known – rose from the streets of Dagenham to head the Church of England is a feat that shows the great strength of character he commands. I had the cheek to write him a letter in which I reminded him of those days by addressing him by his childhood nickname 'Georgie'. He responded that he rather liked being called that because "it reminded him of his mother calling him in for tea after a game in the banjo" (a cul de sac between our homes). He concluded his letter by writing, "That tough, yet very happy background has influenced my ministry, and my life, and possibly yours, more than one can say". Well said, Georgie. It is certainly true that what became of us was more extraordinary than we could have dreamed of on those streets of Dagenham in the 1940s and '50s. If I had known then, as my career stretched before me, just who I would meet and how I would live, I may have been a little in awe of the life that lay ahead, but, of course, I had no way of knowing what would happen anymore than any of my friends did.

AN ANSWER TO THE QUESTION

A few weeks later, Jean and I departed France and England again to set sail for Australia. This time, we would be travelling aboard the *Crystal Symphony* from Dover to Dublin, Belfast, Reykyavik and then on to Greenland and New York, where we would join the *Sun Princess* to return to Brisbane. Sometimes it seems that my life has come full circle. Just like the old days, I now spend almost six months of the year on a cruise ship – although now I don't have to work. The weather was terrible for our cruise on the *Crystal Symphony*, though the ship and its staff couldn't have been more professional. Jean and I whiled away our days, dining sumptuously and taking excellent daily dance lessons with former world champions Tony and Margaret Long.

"Aren't they good," I said to an English couple next to us on the dance floor as we watched Tony and Margaret glide effortlessly around the floor.

"Aren't they ever!" they answered. It didn't take us long to recognise, as we chatted more, that there was something familiar about the couple. Then suddenly it hit me.

"David and Kathy Hearne" I gasped. David played for Barking FC back in the '50s, back when I was just a young reporter with the *Dagenham Post* and had been a close friend, although over the years, we had lost touch. He and Kathy had also made a great success of life, living first in New Zealand and then in the UK, where they made their fortune with a string of Kentucky Friend Chicken restaurants before becoming tax exiles in the Cayman Islands for seven years. Strangely, David had contacted me through Friends Reunited not long before, saying how nice it would be to get together again one day, but with them in the Cayman Islands and us splitting our time between Australia, France and England, at the time it hadn't seemed very likely.

"Terry and Jean Hopley!" David and Kathy were as delighted to meet up with us again as we were with them. "I've often wondered…whatever became of Terry Hopley?" David said, shaking his head in astonishment. Somehow his words triggered the memory of my mother. I grinned as I looked over at Jean and Kathy, hugging each other and chattering away excitedly after all these years, and thought back to my mother's pitiful squawk of "Whatever's going to become of us?" in that air-raid shelter. Of course we made arrangements to see David and Kathy again when they visited Brisbane on another cruise they had planned. But fate was to deal them a terrible blow when out of the blue he was diagnosed with cancer. In just a few short months David was gone.

AND SO LIFE GOES ON

By the year 2009 I had accepted that life had quietened down and that Jean and I would enjoy the rest of our life in peaceful retirement. Then it all started again.

I should have spotted the warning signs when Clare Urwin, publisher of *The Cove* magazine told me she was looking for a way to expand the horizons of what was already the most successful magazine on the Gold Coast. "Get involved in promoting cruises for your readers," I told her. "Just make sure you are the best in the business and you can't fail. Remember you have the unique advantage of being able to promote your holidays in the magazine in the way that no other company can."

Clare asked me to devise and write an itinerary for the first trip for Cove Cruising and within 24 hours she had printed an outstanding brochure and wanted me to take 50 per cent of the business."

And so Cove Cruising and its subsidiary Cove Travel were born. Before I had really gathered my thoughts we had a smart new office in Sanctuary Cove, we took on an outstanding staff and we were up and running.

Our first venture was an ambitious grand European tour featuring an extended stay in the Cotswolds, a cruise through the Mediterranean on the *Silver Wind* and extended stay at Royal Mougins, adjoining my home on the French Riviera.

Terry Hopley was back in business and loving every minute of it. I wrote a couple of articles for the fabulous *The Cove* magazine, hosted a couple of special dinner parties and in no time at all the trip was a sell-out. All that was left was for me to organise it and make sure it turned out to be the trip of a lifetime for the 40 lucky participants.

I thought I would begin by sampling the delights of the *Silver Wind*. I knew Silversea Cruises only too well and knew their product was simply the best but who would turn down the chance of a week in the Med just to make sure they knew I was back on the scene. That cruise turned out to be memorable in more ways than one. I was greeted like a long lost friend by so many of the crew who knew me but it was a chance meeting on my morning walk around the deck that really made the cruise for me.

I saw this debonair, sun-tanned figure striding towards me with a confident swagger I couldn't mistake. Even the little goatee beard didn't fool me. We last stood together in our swimming costumes at Barking Open Air Baths more than half a century before and it was just lovely to be back in the company of another old Dagenham mate, Terry Venables.

Terry and his wife Yvette were sampling their first Silversea cruise and from then on we met up each day around the pool to compare notes on the ups and downs of our respective lives since we left our council houses a lifetime ago.

Terry, of course, went on to play soccer for England, then had a stupendous career as a coach, managing clubs such as Tottenham Hotspur and Barcelona before coaching both England and Australia. He has had more than his share of success but in true Dagenham style it hasn't changed him one bit.

Terry and Yvette shared my view that there would be no better ship to use for our inaugural Cove Cruising trip and I knew it would put the finishing touch to the adventure for my Aussie friends.

The trip, in my not so humble opinion, proved I hadn't lost my touch. But you don't have to take my word for it. My guests presented me with a beautiful leather-bound book and each of them wrote a little note saying how wonderful the trip had been.

How to follow up with a holiday to top that was something of a challenge but the idea came to me on one of my regular long cruises back to Southampton from Brisbane.

First I bounced the idea off my business partner Clare Urwin: "We struck gold with the *Silver Wind* so why don't we follow up with another cruise on the same ship, but this time in the Indian Ocean. And for the land content I rope in my old partner in crime John Batchlor for an adventure in South Africa that just couldn't be found anywhere else."

Clare agreed so once again I was in league with my old friend and honorary brother John planning another trip of a lifetime.

Everything fell into place because my cruise back to the UK visited Mauritius (where we would start our next *Silver Wind* cruise) and gave me the chance to find the right hotel as well as catch up with John at his home in Cape Town.

Our 'recce' cruise was aboard the *Balmoral*, hardly the *Silver Wind*, but a ship full of nostalgia and happy memories. The *Balmoral* also gave Jean and I a chance to further our latest and most challenging past-time … ballroom dancing.

On a previous cruise we had met up with Avril and Terry McCrum, ballroom dance teachers who are very much in demand on cruise ships all over the world. They introduced us to sequence dancing – something we had never heard of – and we were hooked, spending hours each day trying to master the physically and mentally challenging steps of 'Saunter Together', the 'Mayfair Quickstep' and the 'Square Tango'. The four of us had become good friends and they took a shine to John when we caught up with him on a two-day stop-over in Cape Town.

So that just about brings me up to date. As I write this I am back in the UK enjoying life, while Clare, as ever, does a great job back at Sanctuary Cove with both the magazine and Cove Cruising. Both go from strength to strength.

How do you end an autobiography when you feel that even as a septegenerian there is so much that still lies ahead. As my mother used to say "Whatever's going to become of us?"

First published 2013 by
New Holland Publishers Pty Ltd
London • Sydney • Cape Town • Auckland

Garfield House 86–88 Edgware Road London W2 2EA United Kingdom
1/66 Gibbes Street Chatswood NSW 2067 Australia
Wembley Square First Floor Solan Road Gardens Cape Town 8001 South Africa
218 Lake Road Northcote Auckland New Zealand

www.newhollandpublishers.com

A record of this book is held at the British Library and The National Library of Australia.

ISBN 978 1 74257 285 7

Publisher: Patsy Rowe
Senior editor: Simona Hill
Designer: Kimberley Pearce, Tracy Loughlin
Proofreader: Jay Thundercliffe
Production director: Olga Dementiev
Printer: Toppan Leefung Printing Ltd

10 9 8 7 6 5 4 3 2 1
Keep up with New Holland Publishers on Facebook http://www.facebook.com/
NewHollandPublishers

UK £14.99